HOWARD BRENTON

Howard Brenton was born in Portsmouth in 1942. His many plays include *Christie in Love* (Portable Theatre, 1969); *Revenge* (Theatre Upstairs, 1969); *Magnificence* (Royal Court Theatre, 1973); *The Churchill Play* (Nottingham Playhouse, 1974, and twice revived by the RSC, 1978 and 1988); *Bloody Poetry* (Foco Novo, 1984, and Royal Court Theatre, 1987); *Weapons of Happiness* (National Theatre, Evening Standard Award, 1976); *Epsom Downs* (Joint Stock Theatre, 1977); *Sore Throats* (RSC, 1978); *The Romans in Britain* (National Theatre, 1980, revived at the Crucible Theatre, Sheffield, 2006); *Thirteenth Night* (RSC, 1981); *The Genius* (1983), *Greenland* (1988) and *Berlin Bertie* (1992), all presented by the Royal Court; *Kit's Play* (RADA Jerwood Theatre, 2000); *Paul* (National Theatre, 2005); *In Extremis* (Shakespeare's Globe, 2006 and 2007); *Never So Good* (National Theatre, 2008); *The Ragged Trousered Philanthropists* adapted from the novel by Robert Tressell (Liverpool Everyman and Chichester Festival Theatre, 2010) and *Anne Boleyn* (Shakespeare's Globe, 2010 and 2011).

Collaborations with other writers include *Brassneck* (with David Hare, Nottingham Playhouse, 1972); *Pravda* (with David Hare, National Theatre, Evening Standard Award, 1985) and *Moscow Gold* (with Tariq Ali, RSC, 1990).

Versions of classics include *The Life of Galileo* (1980) and *Danton's Death* (1982) both for the National Theatre, Goethe's *Faust* (1995/6) for the RSC and a new version of *Danton's Death* for the National Theatre (2010).

He wrote thirteen episodes of the BBC1 drama series *Spooks* (2001–05, BAFTA Best Drama Series, 2003).

Other Titles in this Series

Howard Brenton
ANNE BOLEYN
BERLIN BERTIE
FAUST – PARTS ONE & TWO
    after Goethe
IN EXTREMIS
NEVER SO GOOD
PAUL
THE RAGGED TROUSERED
    PHILANTHROPISTS *after* Tressell

Jez Butterworth
JERUSALEM
JEZ BUTTERWORTH PLAYS: ONE
MOJO
THE NIGHT HERON
PARLOUR SONG
THE RIVER
THE WINTERLING

Caryl Churchill
BLUE HEART
CHURCHILL PLAYS: THREE
CHURCHILL: SHORTS
CLOUD NINE
DING DONG THE WICKED
A DREAM PLAY
    after Strindberg
DRUNK ENOUGH TO SAY
    I LOVE YOU?
FAR AWAY
HOTEL
ICECREAM
LIGHT SHINING IN
    BUCKINGHAMSHIRE
LOVE AND INFORMATION
MAD FOREST
A NUMBER
SEVEN JEWISH CHILDREN
THE SKRIKER
THIS IS A CHAIR
THYESTES *after* Seneca
TRAPS

David Edgar
ALBERT SPEER
ARTHUR & GEORGE
    after Barnes
CONTINENTAL DIVIDE
EDGAR: SHORTS
THE MASTER BUILDER
    after Ibsen
PENTECOST
THE PRISONER'S DILEMMA
THE SHAPE OF THE TABLE
TESTING THE ECHO
A TIME TO KEEP
    with Stephanie Dale
WRITTEN ON THE HEART

Debbie Tucker Green
BORN BAD
DIRTY BUTTERFLY
RANDOM
STONING MARY
TRADE & GENERATIONS
TRUTH AND RECONCILIATION

Ayub Khan-Din
EAST IS EAST
LAST DANCE AT DUM DUM
NOTES ON FALLING LEAVES
RAFTA, RAFTA...

Liz Lochhead
BLOOD AND ICE
DRACULA *after* Bram Stoker
EDUCATING AGNES ('The School
    for Wives') *after* Molière
GOOD THINGS
LIZ LOCHHEAD: FIVE PLAYS
MARY QUEEN OF SCOTS GOT
    HER HEAD CHOPPED OFF
MEDEA *after* Euripides
MISERYGUTS & TARTUFFE
    after Molière
PERFECT DAYS
THEBANS

Conor McPherson
DUBLIN CAROL
McPHERSON PLAYS: ONE
McPHERSON PLAYS: TWO
PORT AUTHORITY
THE SEAFARER
SHINING CITY
THE VEIL
THE WEIR

Enda Walsh
BEDBOUND & MISTERMAN
DELIRIUM
DISCO PIGS & SUCKING DUBLIN
ENDA WALSH PLAYS: ONE
MISTERMAN
THE NEW ELECTRIC BALLROOM
PENELOPE
THE SMALL THINGS
THE WALWORTH FARCE

Nicholas Wright
CRESSIDA
HIS DARK MATERIALS *after* Pullman
THE LAST OF THE DUCHESS
MRS KLEIN
THE REPORTER
THÉRÈSE RAQUIN *after* Zola
TRAVELLING LIGHT
VINCENT IN BRIXTON
WRIGHT: FIVE PLAYS

Howard Brenton

55 DAYS

NICK HERN BOOKS
London
www.nickhernbooks.co.uk

A Nick Hern Book

55 Days first published in Great Britain as a paperback original in 2012 by Nick Hern Books Limited, The Glasshouse, 49a Goldhawk Road, London W12 8QP, in association with Hampstead Theatre, London

55 Days copyright © 2012 Howard Brenton

Howard Brenton has asserted his right to be identified as the author of this work

Cover image by SWD (www.swd.uk.com) with Mark Gatiss as Charles I
Cover design by Ned Hoste, 2H

Typeset by Nick Hern Books, London
Printed in Great Britain by CPI Group (UK) Ltd

A CIP catalogue record for this book is available from the British Library

ISBN 978 1 84842 287 2

55 Days was first performed at Hampstead Theatre, London, on 18 October 2012, with the following cast:

LADY FAIRFAX	Abigail Cruttenden
GENERAL IRETON	Daniel Flynn
THOMAS HARRISON	Matthew Flynn
KING CHARLES I	Mark Gatiss
ROBERT HAMMOND	Richard Henders
OLIVER CROMWELL	Douglas Henshall
LORD FAIRFAX	Simon Kunz
JOHN LILBURNE	Gerald Kyd
WILLIAM LENTHALL	John MacKay
TROOPER / AXTELL	Jordan Mifsud
TROOPER / COLONEL PRIDE / PRIEST	Gerard Monaco
MARY COOKE	Laura Rogers
JOHN COOKE / LORD GREY / PRYNNE	Tom Vaughan-Lawlor
CHILLENDEN / EXECUTIONER / TROOPER	Jem Wall
DUKE OF RICHMOND / JOHN BRADSHAW	James Wallace

Director	Howard Davies
Designer	Ashley Martin Davis
Lighting Designer	Rick Fisher
Composer	Dominic Muldowney
Sound Designer	Paul Groothuis
Casting	Gemma Hancock and Sam Stevenson

Characters

OLIVER CROMWELL, *Lieutenant General, MP and second-in-command of the Parliamentary Army*
KING CHARLES I
LORD THOMAS FAIRFAX, *Commander-in-Chief of the Parliamentary Army*
LADY ANNE FAIRFAX, *his wife, a Presbyterian*
HENRY IRETON, *General in the Parliamentary Army*
JOHN LILBURNE, *leader of the Levellers, once close to Cromwell*
THOMAS HARRISON, *Major in the Parliamentary Army, a Republican*
ROBERT HAMMOND, *gaoler of the King, once a Royalist*
DUKE OF RICHMOND, *cousin of the King and a Privy Counsellor*
WILLIAM LENTHALL, *Speaker of the House of Commons*
THOMAS PRIDE, *Colonel in the Parliamentary Army*
JOHN COOKE, *lawyer, lead prosecutor at the King's trial*
MARY COOKE, *his wife, a Baptist*
JOHN BRADSHAW, *Judge, President of the High Court at the King's trial*
WILLIAM PRYNNE MP, *leader of the Presbyterians*
EDMUND CHILLENDEN, *ex-soldier, a Leveller*
THREE ARMY TROOPERS
DANIEL AXTELL, *Captain of the Parliamentary Guard, a Baptist*
RICHARD BRANDON, *an executioner*
A PRIEST

And a MESSENGER, SOLDIERS, SPECTATORS

This text went to press before the end of rehearsals and so may differ slightly from the play as performed.

ACT ONE

Scene One

Hyde Park. Night. It is very cold. The Parliamentary Army is encamped. Three TROOPERS *– pikemen from the fens, pikes stacked – huddle before a fire. The* FIRST TROOPER *is in his teens, the other two are veterans.*

FIRST TROOPER. That fire needs a perk-up.

SECOND TROOPER. Best save the wood we have.

FIRST TROOPER. Huh.

They pull their clothing tighter about them then stare at the fire for a while.

There's that fence. Other side of Park Lane.

SECOND TROOPER. No foraging.

FIRST TROOPER. Half of it's gone anyway.

SECOND TROOPER. No foraging.

THIRD TROOPER. What'd be the harm?

SECOND TROOPER. You know the ordinance.

THIRD TROOPER. Ah well, an Army ordinance, well, that's that, there we be. (*A pause.*) Well. (*A pause.*) There.

They stare at the fire for a while.

FIRST TROOPER. Rest of that fence'll be gone by dawn.

THIRD TROOPER. Boy, understand. You cannot steal wood because you are a saint.

FIRST TROOPER. Am I?

THIRD TROOPER. You are! We are all modern saints because we are God's army, fighting for a new Jerusalem.

SECOND TROOPER. New Jerusalem.

THIRD TROOPER. So look around this camp, boy, what do you see? Half-starved soldiers slumped over tiny fires? No no! Men all but at the end of their tether? Wondering why the cause for Parliament and Commonwealth is still not yet won, and after six years of fights and wreckage up and down poor old England? No no no! You see a host of saints! Shining with God's purpose! Unpaid, near to mutiny, but saints!

FIRST TROOPER. And bloody freezing.

SECOND TROOPER. Hey!

THIRD TROOPER. No swearing.

SECOND TROOPER. Army ordinance.

FIRST TROOPER. Why, cos we're saints?

THIRD TROOPER. I do believe the boy is coming to a godly understanding.

The SECOND *and* THIRD TROOPERS *laugh.*

JOHN LILBURNE *enters. He keeps to the shadows. He is about to approach the* TROOPERS *but withdraws into shadow when he sees* GENERAL IRETON *enter, hastening along, head down, avoiding the men.*

LILBURNE. Henry.

IRETON *whirls round, hand on his sword.*

IRETON. John? What are you doing here?

LILBURNE. Come to be with freeborn men.

IRETON. John, go. Before the pickets see you.

LILBURNE. Why is the Army in Hyde Park?

IRETON. None of this concerns you.

LILBURNE. Parliament's Army, moving on the capital? That concerns every freeborn man.

IRETON. If you go agitating amongst the men tonight, so help me God, despite all that's been between us, I'll have the pickets take you to the Fleet in irons.

LILBURNE. 'All that's been between us', Henry? What's that? Brothers in arms against the King's Army at Marston Moor, walking side by side up to death? That the 'that' you mean?

IRETON. Times change.

LILBURNE. Do they?

IRETON. I appeal to you, John.

A pause.

LILBURNE. Have the Commons voted yet?

IRETON. I cannot…

LILBURNE. Just tell me, man! Have they voted for the King's trial?

IRETON. The last dispatcher from Westminster said they are still debating.

LILBURNE. And if the vote goes against the will of the Army Council?

IRETON. We wait upon the hand of the Lord.

LILBURNE. What does Oliver say?

IRETON *stares at him.*

I want to see him.

IRETON. He's not here.

LILBURNE *is taken aback.*

LILBURNE. Not here?

IRETON. John, so help me, if you do not leave this place, I will arrest you! Now!

LILBURNE (*steps back*). May God stay your hand tonight, General Ireton.

IRETON. No, may He move it.

LILBURNE *backs away into the dark.* IRETON *exits. The* TROOPERS *stare at the fire for a while.*

SECOND TROOPER. Saw Old Ironsides catch a man foraging. Before the fight at Marston Moor. Eggs, six eggs, that's all, stolen from some farm. Dear Lord, what he did to that man.

FIRST TROOPER. What, he hit him?

SECOND TROOPER. Far, far worse. He used words. It were like he tore out that thief's soul and threw it down. I swear I saw his soul die there before us, on the grass. Then Ol' Ironsides told him to go and never return to the Army.

THIRD TROOPER. And where is he now?

SECOND TROOPER. Who knows? Some corner of Hell, eating eggs for eternity?

The FIRST TROOPER *laughs.*

THIRD TROOPER. I mean Old Ironsides. Where is our Lieutenant General Oliver Cromwell?

Unease.

FIRST TROOPER. I heard say he's still in the north.

THIRD TROOPER. The fighting in the north's all but done.

SECOND TROOPER. He'll be here with us.

THIRD TROOPER. Tell you what I think…

SECOND TROOPER. I don't care to know what you think!

THIRD TROOPER. I think…

WILLIAM LENTHALL *crosses the stage quickly, protecting his head against the rain.*

FIRST TROOPER (*interrupting the* THIRD TROOPER). Who's that?

SECOND TROOPER. I know him, he was good to me once. Speaker Lenthall. Mr Speaker, God be with you!

LENTHALL. And with you, trooper! (*Stops.*) Is it Michael Savage?

SECOND TROOPER. Yes, Mr Speaker.

LENTHALL. Glad to see you in health, Michael.

THIRD TROOPER. Master Lenthall, have the Commons voted?

LENTHALL. They have.

THIRD TROOPER. And how?

LENTHALL. Against the motion.

The TROOPERS *are lost.*

SECOND TROOPER. Against?

LENTHALL. Against bringing the King to trial.

SECOND TROOPER. But how can that be?

THIRD TROOPER. By what number of votes?

LENTHALL. Eighty-three for the King to be tried. One
hundred and twenty-nine against.

SECOND TROOPER. How can that be?

THIRD TROOPER. It's the Presbyterians…

SECOND TROOPER. In the name of God and all His Saints,
how can that be!?

LENTHALL. Free men in Parliament freely cast their votes.

THIRD TROOPER. The Presbyterians.

LENTHALL. A free vote in a free Parliament, is that not what
we've fought for all these years?

SECOND TROOPER. Aye, but not in a Parliament of fanatics!

LENTHALL *(turns on him)*. Respect the Commons, Michael!

SECOND TROOPER. I'll respect the House of Commons but
not the men in it!

THIRD TROOPER. The Presbyterians will bring back the
King's tyranny!

LENTHALL. Trooper, we must pray for a settlement in these
matters.

THIRD TROOPER. There's only one settlement for Charles
Stuart. *(Gesture across his throat.)*

LENTHALL. Hush now. That's treason.

THIRD TROOPER. The treason's all with Charles Stuart! At war with the people of England these past six years!

LENTHALL. MPs shouting at me, now it's soldiers, it's the night for it!

He exits.

THIRD TROOPER. Dear God above, help us, we're going in.

SECOND TROOPER. No.

THIRD TROOPER. The Army Council moved us down into London to frighten the MPs. But they've not took fright. We're going in.

SECOND TROOPER. Oliver will never let that happen.

THIRD TROOPER. But he's not here, is he!

FIRST TROOPER. Going in where?

SECOND TROOPER. Into Parliament.

FIRST TROOPER. To do what?

THIRD TROOPER. Arrest the MPs who won't vote for the King's trial.

FIRST TROOPER. But we're… we're Parliament's Army. Sworn to protect Parliament. How can we go and fight it?

THIRD TROOPER. It's called politics, boy.

LORD THOMAS FAIRFAX *enters. He loops across the stage. The* SECOND TROOPER *stands at once.*

SECOND TROOPER. Look to yourselves.

TROOPERS *stand, hands raised in greeting – not salutes.*

TROOPERS. My Lord Commander! / My Lord! / God be with you, My Lord!

FAIRFAX. And with all of us, this night.

SECOND TROOPER. My Lord, we have heard of the vote.

FAIRFAX. The Devil gives bad news wings.

THIRD TROOPER. Are we to move against Parliament, My Lord?

All are still.

FAIRFAX. We are to look to our prayers, trooper. There lies our guidance.

TROOPERS. Amen.

FAIRFAX *turns away.* IRETON, *entering, waylays him.*

IRETON. My Lord.

FAIRFAX. General Ireton.

IRETON. We must not delay…

FAIRFAX *and* IRETON *exit.*

SECOND TROOPER. Lord Thomas Fairfax! Black Tom. A great man.

FIRST TROOPER. He don't look so black. More… sallow.

SECOND TROOPER. What?

FIRST TROOPER. His skin. Looks sallow.

SECOND TROOPER. If you had the burden of that man, you'd have no skin left on at all. Be a walkin' skeleton.

THIRD TROOPER. I never stomached an aristocrat-cum-landowner commanding God-fearing common men.

SECOND TROOPER. I tell you that man has the wrath of God within him. Marston Moor…

THIRD TROOPER. I remember.

FIRST TROOPER. I wish I'd been at that battle.

SECOND TROOPER. No you don't.

FIRST TROOPER. God would have been with me. The Lord is our light.

The two veterans look at each other.

SECOND TROOPER. Aye, boy. Praise be to Him.

FIRST TROOPER. Amen.

SECOND TROOPER. Amen.

THIRD TROOPER. Amen.

> JOHN LILBURNE *comes quickly out of the dark and joins them.*

LILBURNE. Good evening, gentlemen.

SECOND TROOPER. What are you doing here?

LILBURNE. Making trouble, trooper.

> *A flicker of grim humour from the* TROOPERS.

I think we met at Putney. Michael Savage?

SECOND TROOPER. It is.

> *They shake hands.*

LILBURNE (*to the* THIRD TROOPER). Matthew.

THIRD TROOPER. John. (*Does not offer his hand.*)

LILBURNE (*to the* FIRST TROOPER). Lad. (*Hand out.*) John Lilburne.

FIRST TROOPER. John… John Lil… Freeborn John?

LILBURNE. I'd call every man and woman freeborn. What's your name, lad?

FIRST TROOPER. William Bond.

LILBURNE. Freeborn Bill, then. For the fire. (*Takes wood out from under his coat.*)

SECOND TROOPER. Where did you get that?

LILBURNE. Fence over by Park Lane.

> *The* SECOND TROOPER *is cross. The* THIRD TROOPER *laughs. The* FIRST TROOPER *takes the wood enthusiastically and puts it on the fire.*

SECOND TROOPER. You were an officer in this Army, a field-promoted Lieutenant General! You should not urge a recruit to go against ordinances… you should not do that!

LILBURNE. I'm a citizen now, scavenging along with the rest.

SECOND TROOPER. A pretty pass, to hear Freeborn John call himself a scavenger.

LILBURNE. It is a pretty pass that we have all come to. So who gave the order to come into London?

A reluctance.

My Lord Fairfax? (*A moment.*) Oliver?

THIRD TROOPER. It were General Ireton.

LILBURNE. With Oliver's agreement?

THIRD TROOPER. No, it were Ireton on his own say.

SECOND TROOPER (*to the* THIRD TROOPER). We shouldn't talk of this.

LILBURNE. So, what? Oliver's still in the north? What's up there to busy him, when there's all this tumult in London?

SECOND TROOPER. Old Ironsides knows what he's doing.

LILBURNE. Does he? Do you?

Unease.

I tell you what I fear. That you are going to attack Parliament. Because it will not do the Army's will.

SECOND TROOPER. Orders are orders.

LILBURNE. No man should obey an order he thinks unjust.

SECOND TROOPER. Easily said.

LILBURNE. Remember why the King launched these wars against his people. And why we fought back! For a free England with a free Parliament. (*Lower.*) If the Army Council orders you to move against the House of Commons, you must not obey. They are all landowners, grandees, they act for their own purposes, for their estates and big houses, not for you and your families. You know this.

THIRD TROOPER. John, time was I listened to your talk of levelling men to equals. And maybe I'll listen again, maybe all of us will. But not now.

LILBURNE. Why not?

THIRD TROOPER. Cos Parliament has let us down! And needs a bloody nose!

LILBURNE. This Army was made by Parliament to protect its liberties.

THIRD TROOPER. And when those liberties are used for tyranny? What then?

SECOND TROOPER. Hang a few MPs.

The FIRST TROOPER *laughs.*

LILBURNE. Boy, you do not know what you're laughing at.

FIRST TROOPER. I'm laughing for the rights of the common man.

SECOND TROOPER. Well said.

LILBURNE. How has this all got so twisted?

THIRD TROOPER. The days of dreaming of all with equal rights have to wait, John. We've got a fight here.

LILBURNE. Matthew, destroy a freely voting Commons and those days will never come! All will fall to barbarity, cruelty, greater tyranny. In the name of our sweet Saviour Jesus Christ, I beg you, refuse your orders.

THIRD TROOPER. Wrongs and rights? All I know is there's a fight against a King and we must win it.

LILBURNE. You were a good man, Matthew.

THIRD TROOPER. We were all good men, when these wars began.

LILBURNE. I've not changed.

THIRD TROOPER. No, you've not.

Drums. The TROOPERS *stand. They stamp the fire out, take up weapons.*

John. Go.

SECOND TROOPER. Go.

LILBURNE. Don't do this!

VOICE. The Army will take up weapons and form to lines!

VOICES. Weapons and to lines!

LILBURNE. Make a stand, others will follow…

THIRD TROOPER. Goodbye, John.

Shouts, noise. LILBURNE *exits into darkness and the camp is hurriedly breaking up.*

End of Scene One.

Scene Two

A corridor in Westminster.

A cacophony of VOICES, *off, shouting: 'Privilege! Privilege! / Mr Speaker! Mr Speaker! / Order order…'*

The three TROOPERS *enter dragging* WILLIAM PRYNNE *along. He is resisting with all his might and shouting.*

PRYNNE*'s ears and his nose have been mutilated – he wears a patch over his nose.*

PRYNNE. Privilege of Parliament!

THIRD TROOPER. Mr Prynne, you are under arrest.

PRYNNE. Privilege of Parliament, I claim privilege of Parliament!

FIRST TROOPER. His nose…

PRYNNE. The King cut it off, lad! For defending the liberty of Parliament you deny!

Enter THOMAS HARRISON.

HARRISON. Troopers, let him go.

PRYNNE *starts forward at* HARRISON *as if to hit him but stops.*

PRYNNE. Thomas Harrison, you cannot support this outrage!

HARRISON. But I do. William Prynne, you are purged.

PRYNNE. 'Purged'? What is this 'purged'?

HARRISON. All you Presbyterians are expelled from the House of Commons, you are stripped of your privileges.

PRYNNE. By what authority?

HARRISON. By the agreement of the people in God's Army.

PRYNNE. No, by the force of tyrant generals, who tonight have destroyed a free Parliament!

Enter IRETON *and* FAIRFAX. FAIRFAX *keeps his distance.*

HARRISON. You voted down the King's trial. Why? Because you have secret dealings with him! What did Charles Stuart promise you? What? What?

IRETON. The King promised them he would do away with bishops.

PRYNNE. I see you, Ireton. You ordered soldiers with swords drawn into the Commons! This rape of Parliament is your doing!

HARRISON. Confess that you dealt with Charles Stuart!

IRETON. Yes, Prynne, confess your treason.

PRYNNE. Oh, I confess, I confess that bishops are an abomination!

FAIRFAX (*to* IRETON). Oh, that sound of rant.

IRETON. The curse of our times.

PRYNNE. Bishops blight the land, they corrupt, they ruin farmers with their rents, they lounge in their palaces with stuffed bellies, rubies on their fat fingers, above all they stand between men and women and their God! The King has agreed to abolish them. If he is doing God's work, why should he be tried for his life?

HARRISON. Charles Stuart will never abolish bishops, he's damn well near a Papist.

PRYNNE. His Majesty has given me his word.

IRETON. Oh, his word. Well, there's a marvel.

HARRISON. The man who had your face cut to bits because of your religion, now you trust his word?

PRYNNE. I am against the King in religion, but not against him as a sovereign power! And I believe the word of my Sovereign.

HARRISON. Parliament is sovereign. The King denies it. Give him power again and he will sweep away all of us: all the factions, you and your Presbyterians, me, the Army, Levellers, Diggers, dreamers, and with us all the liberties Parliament has won in these bitter wars. That man of blood must be brought to trial.

LENTHALL *enters*.

PRYNNE. You are a republican, Harrison. You want no King at all!

LENTHALL. All who were on the list have been removed from the Commons and I have suspended the session.

IRETON. Troopers, take your prisoner away.

PRYNNE. Send for Cromwell, he will not allow this, he will defend the rights of Parliament!

HARRISON. Troopers, come.

PRYNNE. Where is he? Where is he? Where is Cromwell?

HARRISON. Now!

PRYNNE. Where's Cromwell? Send for Cromwell!

Exit the TROOPERS, *manhandling* PRYNNE *and* HARRISON.

LENTHALL, IRETON *and* FAIRFAX *remain*.

LENTHALL. Well, sirs, a good night's work.

IRETON. Indeed, Mr Speaker.

LENTHALL. I must look through the list of the MPs who are arrested. Inform the Fleet Prison of those who should be held and…

A moment.

IRETON. Yes.

Then LENTHALL *exits.*

FAIRFAX. Have we really just done this thing? Have we really attacked Parliament?

IRETON. No. We have attacked the enemies of Parliament.

FAIRFAX. We have destroyed the very thing we fought to make!

IRETON. No. We have purged it.

FAIRFAX. That hateful word.

IRETON. It is a good word, a medical word, purged as in 'rid the body of nauseous matter'.

FAIRFAX. I am so tired.

IRETON. We are all *tired*, Thomas. The whole country is *tired*. We had no choice in this! Prynne and his lunatics were going to give power back to the King.

FAIRFAX. Some see Prynne as a God-fearing Christian.

IRETON. You mean like your wife?

FAIRFAX. Be careful, General Ireton, I am your commanding officer.

IRETON. Then… (*Shuts up.*)

FAIRFAX. What? Command? I did! I forbade you to bring the Army into London!

IRETON. Then why don't you cashier me? But you and I know why. The Army has its own mind, we would have had a mutiny if we had not moved against Prynne! Neither you nor I could have stopped that.

FAIRFAX. Oliver could have.

IRETON. Then where is he? That voice, that mind to which we defer, the leader the Lord Himself has given us? Or so some say.

FAIRFAX. I say.

IRETON. I too, I too... God's Englishman...

FAIRFAX. Which he has proved to be again and again...

IRTON. Yes yes! But at this crucial time, God's own is not here, is he!

FAIRFAX. Then damn my bloody eyes, I'll go and get him!

They stare at each other, near to blows. Then they calm down. IRETON *grins.*

IRETON. Swearing, Commander?

FAIRFAX. Someone has to, amongst all these saints. I'll set out for Pontefract tonight. (*Turning away.*)

IRETON. Tell Oliver: I did the Lord's work.

FAIRFAX. Did you?

End of Scene Two.

Scene Three

*Carisbrooke Castle, the Isle of Wight. Bowling green. A jack
and five bowls are on the stage. A sixth rolls on, bumping into
the others.*

RICHMOND (*off*). Oh, played, played, Your Majesty!

Enter KING CHARLES I *and a courtier, the* DUKE OF
RICHMOND.

CHARLES. Yes, I have it!

RICHMOND. You do, you do, Sire.

*RICHMOND kicks the balls into two groups. He picks up the
jack and gives it to CHARLES. He considers for a moment
then rolls the jack off the stage. They consider the jack's
position.*

Going long on this leg, Your Majesty?

CHARLES. It is to stretch you, Richmond.

Enter ROBERT HAMMOND. *He waits. He is uneasy.*
CHARLES *ignores him.*

RICHMOND. Sire, your gaoler waits upon you.

CHARLES. Yes, look: his shadow on the grass? See it as the
gibbet he will one day hang from. (*A smile.*) Colonel
Hammond. Thank you for the fresh eggs at breakfast.

HAMMOND. They were sent by a farmer near Ventnor.

CHARLES. So, there is still one farmer in England who has not
raised units of horse and pikemen against his Sovereign?

HAMMOND. Your Majesty… (*Hesitates.*) There is news.

CHARLES. Ah. Is Oliver Cromwell hanged?

RICHMOND. The vote in Parliament?

HAMMOND. Yes.

RICHMOND. Well, come on, man!

HAMMOND. They voted against His Majesty being put on trial.

CHARLES *and* RICHMOND *stare at him*.

RICHMOND. In what number?

HAMMOND. Eighty-three for, one hundred and twenty-nine against.

A pause.

Then CHARLES *and* RICHMOND *begin to laugh.*

RICHMOND. The Presbyterians. They voted for Your Majesty.

CHARLES. Yes.

RICHMOND. They believed you.

CHARLES. Why should they not? Their Sovereign made them a promise.

HAMMOND. Your Majesty…

RICHMOND. Leave us.

HAMMOND. I…

RICHMOND. Will you forever snoop and pry and stand in His Majesty's hearing?

HAMMOND *bows, withdraws, but hovers.*

RICHMOND. Your Majesty. There is danger in this.

CHARLES. I see only the hand of Almighty God.

RICHMOND. But you promised the Presbyterians you would abolish bishops!

CHARLES. And they promised full restoration of the sovereign power given to me by Heaven. And taken from me by treasonable rebels in these wars! What is the difficulty?

RICHMOND. The difficulty… forgive me for being bold, Your Majesty… When Your Majesty is free and with your powers restored, as Head of the Church of England, will you abolish bishops?

CHARLES. Of course not, don't be absurd.

RICHMOND. And what of the Presbyterians?

CHARLES. Put them in gaol and cut off their noses? I have before. Disgusting little men with red eyes, shouting about religion. And Her Majesty the Queen could never bear the sight of the appalling clothes they wear. (*Laughs*.)

RICHMOND. So the promise...

CHARLES. Black cloth, strong body odour, spittle down their fronts from too much preaching... (*Laughs again*.)

RICHMOND. So Your Majesty's promise...

CHARLES. What does it matter what I say to rebels? Presbyterians, Cromwell, the generals, the agitators... they will all hang. That is my promise.

RICHMOND *is about to speak but* HAMMOND *strides forward*.

HAMMOND. Your Majesty...

RICHMOND. In Hell's name, man!

HAMMOND. I should not tell you this. I should not tell Your Majesty anything.

CHARLES. Robyn, I appreciate your courtesy. Please.

A moment.

HAMMOND. After the vote, the Army purged the Parliament.

All still.

RICHMOND. Purged?

HAMMOND. An MP, Thomas Harrison, called for the suspension of the House. Then troopers under the command of a Colonel Pride invaded the Chamber. All who had voted against... against the motion... were barred. Those who resisted were arrested.

RICHMOND. The Army has attacked Parliament?

CHARLES. Rebellion turns matricide.

RICHMOND. Now they can do anything.

CHARLES. That Harrison I know of. A rebel with his neck marked long ago. But Colonel Pride?

RICHMOND. The Army generals sent a nonentity to do their dirty work.

CHARLES. That is unlike Cromwell. If there's dirty work, he is always to the fore. That I'll give the man.

HAMMOND. The Lieutenant General is not in London.

A moment.

RICHMOND. Cromwell is not with the Army Council?

HAMMOND. The word is he is still at the siege of Pontefract.

CHARLES (*to* RICHMOND). What does this mean?

RICHMOND. Thank you, Hammond.

HAMMOND. Your Majesty, may I speak?

RICHMOND. You may not.

CHARLES. No, Robyn, what do you wish to say?

HAMMOND. Send a message to Cromwell. The Lieutenant General is not a threat to Your Majesty's person.

CHARLES. Really? After six years of rebellion and wars and so many battles I had formed a contrary impression.

HAMMOND. He seeks only to settle with you.

CHARLES. Does he now.

HAMMOND. Many of your loyal subjects would beg you to settle. (*Hesitates.*) Myself among them.

CHARLES. Indeed? But you are my gaoler. For which, one day, you will be hanged.

A horrible moment.

If I am in an ill temper.

Uneasy laughter.

RICHMOND. That is enough, Hammond.

HAMMOND. Your Majesty, My Lord. Shall I thank the farmer? For the eggs?

They stare at him. HAMMOND *bows and exits.*

CHARLES. A gaoler loyal to his prisoner? Men walk with their heels upwards. Topsy-turvy days.

RICHMOND. Days that have crucified many men's consciences, Sire.

CHARLES. I cannot see why. Did not Christ Himself say 'He who is not for me is against me'?

RICHMOND. But, Sire, consider: Hammond may be right. Cromwell may have stayed in the north because he disapproves of the Army's purge. Perhaps there is friction there. Cromwell has always given short shrift to the wilder rebels. If Your Majesty sent a message to him asking to talk, safely, secretly, perhaps we could split the Army leadership.

CHARLES. Tsk tsk tsk, politics, mere politics, Richmond. No more of that, no more dealings with Parliamentarians, Presbyterians or Cromwell and his so-called 'Independents'. They are all traitors and I will fight them.

RICHMOND. But, Sire, with what? The Scots Army that came south to support you, Cromwell has cut it to pieces. That was your last hope.

CHARLES. Richmond, understand. I can lose and lose, battles, plots, conspiracies. But they have only to lose once. Then Cromwell and the generals are severed heads on London Bridge and their followers corpses on gibbets along every road out of London. That is all I need. One victory.

RICHMOND. Yes, Sire. But why is he still in the north...

A church bell is heard.

CHARLES. Evensong. At least they haven't taken the bell from Carisbrooke Chapel.

RICHMOND. We have Hammond to thank for that.

CHARLES. Yes. But he will hang, you know. With them all. Come, we must pray.

End of Scene Three.

Scene Four

Knottingley. CROMWELL*'s billet in a room above a tavern. A table, chairs.* OLIVER CROMWELL *washes.*

CROMWELL. Lord God of Hosts, in this hour of danger, be with England.

A silence.

Lord? Lord?

He looks up.

A silence. Then he stands and blunders across the room. He steadies himself against a table, breathing heavily.

Enter FAIRFAX.

FAIRFAX. Oliver.

CROMWELL *is still. Then he turns. Great charm.*

CROMWELL. Ah. Thomas. I thought you'd send someone, but not your good self.

FAIRFAX. Did you?

CROMWELL. You must be tired out.

FAIRFAX. I rode the Army posts. It only took a night and a day.

CROMWELL. With four war wounds and rheumatism.

FAIRFAX. Mortality is with us all.

CROMWELL (*calls out*). Sergeant Alton!

A TROOPER *enters at once.*

FAIRFAX. Food and beer for me and the Commander.

TROOPER. Yes, General. (*Exits.*)

CROMWELL. There is still good ale in Yorkshire, though little else.

FAIRFAX. Yes. I saw the condition of the country. I was shocked to the heart.

CROMWELL. We seek to love the Lord and His poor, despised people, to do all we can for them… but what devastation we cause! Have they done it?

FAIRFAX. What do you think?

CROMWELL. Who spoke for the vote in the Chamber?

FAIRFAX. Thomas Harrison.

CROMWELL. Hotly, no doubt. What units were used?

FAIRAX. Colonel Pride and his regiment of foot went into Westminster. Nathaniel Rich and his regiment of horse occupied Parliament Square.

CROMWELL. Pride. A puffed-up cockerel crowing on the Speaker's chair. Well. It is the will of the Army.

FAIRFAX. But not mine! Is it yours? Do you support the purge or not? I cannot believe you ever foresaw Parliament invaded by troopers, but for all I know you ordered it!

CROMWELL. No. I did not.

FAIRFAX. Then, in God's name, I need to know your mind.

CROMWELL. When men become soldiers they are still citizens. The Army has its own mind.

FAIRFAX. We created the Army!

CROMWELL. The Lord created it.

FAIRFAX *is furious and about to speak, but* SERGEANT ALTON *enters with a tray. Two tankards. Bread, cheese.*

FAIRFAX. Thank you, Sergeant.

ALTON. My Lord. Will there be anything else, General?

CROMWELL. I want the horses well groomed. It was all mud and scratches today. I'll inspect them in two hours' time.

ALTON. Yes, General.

The TROOPER *exits.*

CROMWELL. Let me tell you what I saw this morning. I was
out with a company from the Ferrybridge encampment,
what, a mile from Pontefract? There was a skirmish, a group
of the King's Scots fighters sneaking away from the siege.
We cornered them in a scrap of woodland. I called out,
'Lads, lads, don't fight, no cause. You have no cause.' All but
one ran off, dropping their weapons, but that one, he came at
us screeching like a devil. A musketeer fired, he went
down…

A gesture to the top of his arm.

And I saw… it was a boy. What, thirteen? I knelt down to
help the wound, it was not too bad. I asked him where he
was from. Lanark, he said. Lanark, the Scottish Lowlands,
good farming country. 'What are you fighting for, lad?' I
said. 'For good King Charles,' he said. 'And what did King
Charles ever give you?' I asked. 'Five shilling,' he said. 'And
promise of no bishops.'

FAIRFAX. Hunh. The innocent betrayed.

CROMWELL. But I thought: this boy, maybe this is the Lord
coming to our aid! I said, 'If you're a godly lad, go back to
Pontefract, tell your officers they can have safe passage back
to Scotland. Surrender and we can all go back to our farms.'
'Who says so?' he asked. 'Lieutenant General Cromwell says
so,' I replied. And… and…

CROMWELL *falls silent and still.*

FAIRFAX. Yes?

CROMWELL. The horror. On his face. The horror. 'The Devil!'
he shouted, staring at me. 'The Devil's breath on me! The
Devil!' He got to his feet, the musketeer had reloaded. 'No,
don't fire,' I said. 'Let him go.' What do you think, Thomas,
will the boy see his country again, his family farm? If they're
not all starved to death?

FAIRFAX. Oliver…

CROMWELL. The hatred. What can we do about the hatred?

CROMWELL *again falls silent and still.*

FAIRFAX. The truth is, this sad little invasion of the Scots was defeated weeks ago. Pontefract will fall within days. In the name of Heaven, why are you still here?

CROMWELL. I am listening for the voice of providence.

FAIRFAX. Oh good. Any idea when you may hear it?

CROMWELL. How can I? The Lord doesn't send messages saying: 'Oliver, I'm going to talk to you on Thursday, make sure you're not busy.' (*Laughs*.)

FAIRFAX. Don't be coy.

CROMWELL. 'Coy'? Me?

FAIRFAX. What are you really doing, Oliver? Waiting to see which way the wind blows?

   CROMWELL *is taken aback*.

CROMWELL. You think that of me?

FAIRFAX. No, of course not.

CROMWELL. Some think that of me?

FAIRFAX. Some, perhaps…

CROMWELL. Henry Ireton?

   A pause.

   How many times must I say it to you all? In this great enterprise it must be the Lord's will that leads, not us.

FAIRFAX. Oliver, to be frank…

CROMWELL.…oh, be frank, frank!…

FAIRFAX.…while you're sat here in your Yorkshire puddle, waiting for the Almighty to speak to you, the country is falling apart. If you'd been in London, there'd have been no purge.

CROMWELL. You think so?

FAIRFAX. You'd have found a way to defeat the Presbyterians. In Parliament, in politics.

CROMWELL. Would I, now.

FAIRFAX. You have the love and affection of the Army. You would have stopped them going in to the Commons. It's you they follow.

CROMWELL. But to where? I am walking a dark path and who can love to walk in darkness? But often we do, because that is His will.

FAIRFAX. Is chaos His will?

CROMWELL. Yes, if we have sinned.

FAIRFAX. Oliver, you're the most practical man I know. How, at the same time, can you be so… damn religious? I know, I know! I have become the swearing commander of an army that does not swear. Let's eat, I am starving.

They sit at the table. Grace.

CROMWELL. Lord, we thank Thee for Thy bounteous ways seen in the gifts of this table. May we who partake of Thy bounty, be worthy of Thee. Amen.

FAIRFAX. Amen.

They eat for a while, drink beer. FAIRFAX *keeps looking at* CROMWELL – *when will he crack? He does.* CROMWELL *slams his knife down.*

CROMWELL. All right. All right. The politicking, let us do it.

FAIRFAX. Well, now the Presbyterians are removed from Parliament, it is clear that the rump that's left will vote for a trial.

CROMWELL (*laughs*). 'Rump.' Is that what the Parliament of saints has become? An arse to fart hot air?

FAIRFAX. Oliver, a trial of the King will be terrible for this country. There are dangers we cannot imagine.

CROMWELL. Yes, we would enter unknown regions.

FAIRFAX. The problem is that there is such a heat in the Army for a trial…

CROMWELL. Oh, heat and retribution there must be. And Charles Stuart must recognise Parliament's powers. Then the country can ease back into peace, with men and women freely represented, free to worship as they will. (*A pause.*) There will be a way through. To the light. To peace in England. Providence will show it to us.

FAIRFAX. You've been waiting on events, haven't you.

CROMWELL. Waiting on the Lord's word.

FAIRFAX. You wanted the purge.

CROMWELL. I wanted no more of Presbyterians.

FAIRFAX. You wanted the purge. But you didn't know if it would succeed.

CROMWELL. No?

FAIRFAX. So you stayed out of reach, deliberately.

CROMWELL. I have told you! I am in darkness.

FAIRFAX. Then come out of it! Oliver, you really believe the Almighty wants us to put His anointed on trial?

CROMWELL (*scoffs*). 'Anointed'…

FAIRFAX. And if the King is found guilty, then what? What, Oliver?

A pause.

CROMWELL. I plead for revelation.

FAIRFAX. To be blunt: we can't always wait for the divine voice to shout the obvious in your head. We are on the edge of an abyss.

CROMWELL. Very well. (*A moment.*) Very well, we will do a mighty politicking and blunder our way to the light. Order me back to London.

FAIRFAX. Lieutenant General Cromwell, I am ordering you to return to London at once.

CROMWELL. Yes, Commander. Sergeant Alton!

End of Scene Four.

Scene Five

Nag's Head Tavern. Back room.

IRETON, LENTHALL *and* HARRISON.

Cheering is heard offstage.

HARRISON. He's here.

LENTHALL. Now we will know.

> *Enter* CROMWELL *and* FAIRFAX.

> You are as popular as ever, Lieutenant General.

CROMWELL. They would shout as much as if I were going to be hanged.

> *They all look at him. He says nothing.*

HARRISON. Lieutenant General. The purge against Parliament was...

CROMWELL (*interrupts*). New days, new days. There is a serious report from the Isle of Wight?

> *They take a moment to recover from his brusqueness.*

HARRISON. Yes. Spies at Carisbrooke Castle report that the King's companions are urging him to escape.

CROMWELL. Well, when he last attempted that he got stuck in a window. (*Laughs.*) Oh, if only that man's life would dissolve in comedy and ridicule, eh? Imagine a time when no one takes monarchy seriously, and we all just get on with living. Move him. Immediately.

HARRISON. Perhaps... to Hurst Castle?

LENTHALL. A terrible place.

CROMWELL. He must be safe. Hurst Castle will do. Now I wish to speak to General Ireton alone. I have your permission, My Lord?

FAIRFAX (*a moment's hesitation*). Yes, of course.

FAIRFAX, LENTHALL *and* HARRISON *move to go.*

CROMWELL. Thomas. You are to ride to the Isle of Wight to tell the King.

HARRISON. Yes, General.

CROMWELL. Take a good troop of horse with you. Make a clatter when you ride into the courtyard at Carisbrooke. Charles Stuart must feel the seriousness of his predicament.

HARRISON. I will make sure he does, General.

Exit FAIRFAX, LENTHALL *and* HARRISON.

CROMWELL. Henry, are you and I of one mind?

IRETON. I pray so.

CROMWELL. So do I. But are we?

A pause.

If you and I divide, so will the Army. I don't believe Fairfax wants a trial. But there are others who would take the King out into the street and beat him to death with no trial at all. If you and I are not as one, the Army will split and we will all be lost. So we must settle things between us.

IRETON. Whatever happens, Charles Stuart must be tried.

CROMWELL. Yes.

IRETON. You agree?

CROMWELL. That is where the Lord has led.

IRETON. You were not always of that mind.

CROMWELL. New days. So, now we must find how to do this fearsome thing.

IRETON. Great thing.

A pause.

The Army must run the trial.

CROMWELL. No.

IRETON. The demand amongst the men is too strong.

CROMWELL. No, the hotheads in the Army will take control.
We will have anarchy.

IRETON. What then?

CROMWELL. The trial must be run by Parliament.

IRETON. Lilburne and the Levellers will oppose that, bitterly.

CROMWELL. Why? Lilburne is forever defending Parliament.
Why should he object?

IRETON. We purged it. He and his supporters do not trust the
MPs who are left.

CROMWELL. So: the freedom-loving Levellers want a junta of
soldiers to be the court that tries the King? Where is liberty
in that?

IRETON. Everything twists about.

CROMWELL. Yes, men end up arguing for the very thing they
once denounced.

IRETON. Here.

IRETON *holds out a document*.

CROMWELL. What is this?

IRETON. A pamphlet from John Lilburne's printing press, on
the streets tonight.

CROMWELL (*reads*). A new 'Agreement of the People'.

IRETON. It calls for…

CROMWELL. I can guess what it calls for. I know the beauty
of John Lilburne's mind.

IRETON. He will agree to Parliament trying the King. But he
wants a document.

CROMWELL. A new constitution.

IRETON. Asserting the sovereignty of Parliament.

CROMWELL. Which is an excellent thing.

IRETON. The elected Commons to be the supreme authority of England.

CROMWELL. Yes.

IRETON. Elected by universal suffrage amongst all men over the age of twenty-one, whatever their station in life.

CROMWELL. Of course.

IRETON. And forbidding the falling of Parliament's sovereign power into the hands of any other: king, tyrant… (*A moment.*) or general. And he demands that this new constitution be agreed before the King is put on trial.

CROMWELL. Oh, John, free John Lilburne, the future happiness of England shines from you. And you will ruin us all.

CROMWELL *screws up the pamphlet and tosses it away.*

Can't you all… Can't you all see? If we are not as one mind in the matter of the King, now, at this moment, tomorrow we will all stand at Tyburn, looking at our guts in the executioner's fire. It's so… fragile, what we have achieved. Sometimes I freeze within, knowing all can be lost… (*Click of his fingers.*) like that.

A pause.

IRETON. The Army could mutiny over this.

CROMWELL. Then… then we will debate with the Army.

IRETON. You mean let them blow hot air, like the debate at Putney Church.

CROMWELL. If we are to put the King on trial, we must have true agreement, amongst ourselves, in the Army, in Parliament. Are we together in this?

A pause.

IRETON. Yes.

CROMWELL. I'll go and see Lilburne.

IRETON. To say what?

CROMWELL. Who knows? What the Lord leads me to say.

They look at each other.

End of Scene Five.

Scene Six

Carisbrooke Castle. Room.

CHARLES *and* RICHMOND.

CHARLES. Have we heard?

RICHMOND. No, Sire.

CHARLES. The letters were sent?

RICHMOND. Yes…

CHARLES. By Newhaven?

RICHMOND. Sire, the walls…

CHARLES *pauses.*

CHARLES. You sent a man you can trust.

RICHMOND. Your Majesty's matter is well in hand.

CHARLES. Good then. We wait upon Heaven.

RICHMOND. And the Irish.

CHARLES. They are good fighting men. Perhaps a little ferocious. But where has gentlemanly fighting got us?

RICHMOND. The trouble is they are ferociously *Catholic* fighting men.

CHARLES. But loyal.

RICHMOND. Loyal to the plunder they take. Sire, we turned to
fanatical Scots Presbyterians. Now we turn to a horde of
Irish Catholics. There is still time to appeal to the moderates
on the Army Council.

CHARLES. Enough.

RICHMOND. Sire…

CHARLES. Enough! I do not wish your counsel on this,
Richmond. Lord Ormonde will raise an army. And with his
help I will get Cromwell and Fairfax and Ireton and all their
gang into the field one more time. And we will see the will of
Almighty God triumphant at last.

RICHMOND. Your Majesty.

But CHARLES *is uneasy. A pause.*

CHARLES. This is a terrible place. That smell from the privy,
can nothing be done?

RICHMOND. Hammond has offered pomanders.

CHARLES. Pomanders! Ha! Am I to sniff oranges to wipe out
the stench of this age? (*Low.*) Do you think the Duke of
Ormonde can raise enough men?

RICHMOND *about to speak.*

No! No. The walls, the stinking walls.

Clatter and noises, off. Enter HAMMOND, HARRISON
and TROOPERS.

You come in unannounced.

HARRISON. I do. Unannounced. I have a commission.

CHARLES. What is your name?

HARRISON. Major Thomas Harrison.

CHARLES. Harrison? The Republican? Who called me a man
of blood?

HARRISON. I have that privilege.

RICHMOND. Sir, you will address His Majesty correctly!

CHARLES *waves at* RICHMOND *to be quiet.*

CHARLES. Are you come to kill me?

HARRISON. No, that would be unlawful.

CHARLES. Ah, so I am safe.

HARRISON. I am to move you to Hurst Castle.

RICHMOND. But that place is even…

CHARLES *again silences him.*

CHARLES. When are we to be 'moved'?

HARRISON. Tonight. I will escort you. With as little delay as possible… sir.

CHARLES. Oh, I am to be 'sir', am I?

HARRISON. I will treat you as a gentleman.

CHARLES. But I am more than a man. You have no idea, Major, what that means. To be so much more than a man in the eye of God.

HARRISON. We are all equal before God.

CHARLES. All but one.

HARRISON. So say all tyrants.

RICHMOND *starts forward then stops. All still.*

CHARLES. You are rude, sir.

HARRISON. I… I apologise.

CHARLES. Ah, now. And you think that will do you some good?

HARRISON. I will give you some time. We can move at daylight.

CHARLES. That is generous of you, Major Harrison.

HARRISON. Not at all, Your… sir.

He turns to go.

End of Scene Six.

Scene Seven

FAIRFAX *and* CROMWELL. FAIRFAX *with* CROMWELL*'s crumpled copy of the 'Agreement of the People'.*

CROMWELL. So you will do it?

FAIRFAX. Why me? Why not you?

CROMWELL. Because you are the Commander of the Army. You are the mountain. The rest of us are squabbling in the valley.

FAIRFAX. Oh, don't try flattery on me, Oliver, not after all these years.

CROMWELL. No. Foolish of me. (*Smiles.*) But you must chair the debate with the Army.

FAIRFAX. 'Must'? (*Indicates the document.*) You have argued this with Lilburne?

CROMWELL. Oh yes, prettily, merrily, tossed to and fro. I've just come from him.

FAIRFAX. You can still talk with that madman?

CROMWELL. Oh, I always talk of many things with Freeborn John. Tonight we began with my headaches and his stomach cramps. He lives off bread and milk, and doesn't sleep. Turbulent innards in turbulent times. (*Laughs.*)

FAIRFAX. Presumably you then moved on to the pains of the country.

CROMWELL. To and fro.

FAIRFAX. What did you say to him?

> CROMWELL *stares at him.*

> (*The document.*) About this?

> *Nothing from* CROMWELL.

Have you made promises to Lilburne and the Levellers?
Secretly? Promises that we cannot keep?

CROMWELL. Study the document. In detail. Be ready.

FAIRFAX. What, are you my schoolmaster now?

For a moment, FAIRFAX *thinks* CROMWELL *is going to
hit him.*

CROMWELL. What is it in you, Thomas? It's not fear. It's not
weakness.

FAIRFAX. Never threaten me, Oliver. Never.

CROMWELL. Oh, my dear friend, you said we are on the edge
of an abyss? Well, we are over it and falling. We learn to fly,
now, or…

Enter LADY ANNE FAIRFAX. *She has a small pamphlet in
her hand.*

Lady Anne.

ANNE. General Cromwell.

CROMWELL *bows stiffly to her and exits.*

Thomas?

He stares at the document.

Thomas?

He looks up at her.

FAIRFAX. Anne, forgive me, did we wake you?

ANNE. You know I can't sleep, these dangerous nights.

FAIRFAX. No. Some food, some wine with me…

She shakes her head.

Maybe I should sleep, and all the Army commanders, the
MPs shouting in the Commons should sleep, the troopers,
the King, his courtiers, his gaolers, all of us, just for a few
hours, all of the factions, sleep, to wake and say, 'In the
name of God what are we doing to our country?'

ANNE. Wild talk, Thomas.

FAIRFAX. Wild days.

ANNE. I was praying by our bed and a man came in to the room.

FAIRFAX. Man?

ANNE. He came into the room.

FAIRFAX. Anne, what are you talking about, what man?

ANNE. He was holding something out in his hands. You know what it was?

FAIRFAX. No, how can I…

ANNE. It was your head. (*A moment.*) I'd fallen asleep, just for a moment. It was a dream. But do you think he was an angel?

FAIRFAX. We reformers don't believe in angels.

ANNE. Pilate's wife, she had a dream, it made her tell her husband not to do a terrible thing.

FAIRFAX. He was going to kill Christ!

ANNE. And you are going to kill…

They stare at each other for a moment.

FAIRFAX. It won't come to that. Never, I promise you, never. (*Points at the pamphlet in her hand.*) What is that?

ANNE. Mr Prynne's pamphlet: 'Memento to the Present Unparliamentary Junto.'

FAIRFAX. If he continues this rabble-rousing against the Army, we'll have to arrest him again.

ANNE. Well, the King cut off his ears and then a bit of his nose. I suppose you can go all of the hog and cut off his head. For that could be a pastime soon, I think, cutting off heads.

FAIRFAX. Stop that, just stop that.

ANNE. William Prynne is a gentle, God-fearing man.

FAIRFAX. God-fearing he may be, but gentle he is not.

ANNE. He knows Christ's word.

FAIRFAX. He is a dangerous lunatic!

ANNE. He is my co-religionist.

FAIRFAX. Yes, yes. (*A moment.*) Yes.

A pause.

ANNE. And what is *that*?

FAIRFAX. 'The Agreement of the People.'

ANNE. That Leveller monstrosity.

FAIRFAX. They have asked me to oversee the Army and Parliament debate it at Whitehall.

ANNE. So John Lilburne is to have his way? We are all to be reduced to dirty, common democrats?

FAIRFAX. It is the basis for a new constitution. Once that is agreed, we can decide how to treat the King.

ANNE. You'll put His Majesty on trial.

FAIRFAX. That won't happen. A new constitution will involve the monarchy.

ANNE. But the Army demands a trial. Many of them want an execution.

FAIRFAX. No, no…

ANNE. Thomas, the King is against what I believe in religion. But surely it is wrong in the eyes of God to kill him.

FAIRFAX. I told you, woman, it will not come to that!

ANNE. It will.

FAIRFAX. No!

ANNE. Why?

FAIRFAX. Because Oliver will find a way through.

ANNE. Oh, Oliver Cromwell will save the King!

FAIRFAX. Yes.

ANNE. Why, why are you so certain of that?

FAIRFAX. Because he wants liberty, under a monarchy which is not tyrannical. That's what we fought for. He is a moderate man. Ferocious, but moderate.

ANNE. You mean moderate at times but at others a beast? What is Cromwell's power over so many of you? He's not Commander of the Army. He's not an aristocrat, he's barely a gentleman. He has no office of state. He's just one uncouth voice amongst many.

FAIRFAX. Many of us believe that he hears the voice of providence.

ANNE. God speaks through him?

A pause.

FAIRFAX. Yes.

ANNE. 'God's Englishman.' That is so dangerous.

End of Scene Seven.

Scene Eight

[*Note. John Evelyn, on witnessing the Whitehall Debate, said: 'Do these young, raw, ill-spoken men run the country?'*]

Whitehall.

FAIRFAX, LENTHALL, IRETON, HARRISON, LILBURNE, CROMWELL. *Also* COLONEL PRIDE, EDMUND CHILLENDEN *and* LORD GREY.

Many papers.

The debate is chaired by FAIRFAX.

They are standing, shouting, throwing papers in the air. FAIRFAX *sits, despairing.* CROMWELL *remains seated, detached.*

LILBURNE. No other power in the land!

IRETON. We did not agree that!

LILBURNE. It is published! It is set!

IRETON. The document is merely for debate!

FAIRFAX. Gentlemen…

LILBURNE. There must be no other power in the land but Parliament! Voting freely!

GREY. What of the King?

LILBURNE. Strip him of all powers. If not of something else.

CHILLENDEN *and* GREY *laugh*.

CHILLENDEN. Freeborn John!

GREY. God be with you, John!

CHILLENDEN. No cheating the people of their right!

PRIDE / CHILLENDEN / GREY (*chant and clap*). Freeborn John! Freeborn John!

FAIRFAX. Silence! I am ordering you to be silent! And to sit!

PRIDE. Drag the King from his castle and beat him to death!

FAIRFAX. Colonel Pride, sit! And be silent! That is an order.

They all sit.

You are officers and men of the Parliamentary Army. You will not speak so rawly and so ill. I remind you: we are here to fix upon a final settlement between Parliament and His Majesty the King, for the protection of the people's liberties and the peace of this Kingdom.

A silence.

IRETON. There must be remnants of the ancient constitution, there must be restraints on Parliament's power. Rights must be protected.

LILBURNE. The rights of landowners.

CHILLENDEN. What restraints?

IRETON (*hesitates for a moment*). New reponsiblities for the King.

CHILLENDEN. What?

GREY. What?

LILBURNE. What 'responsibilities'?

IRETON. Certain powers.

LILBURNE. What 'powers'?

IRETON. Moderate powers. Limited by law. Checks and balances.

GREY. 'Checks'? 'Balances'?

IRETON. For a new monarchy…

CHILLENDEN.… 'new monarchy'?…

IRETON. That is constitutional.

GREY. I know not what kind of fish or fowl that could be!

IRETON. It will be a monarchy that acknowledges Parliament's supremacy. King and people bound together, legally.

LILBURNE. So much blood, to end up bound to a man in a palace?

CHILLENDEN. Disgraceful.

PRIDE (*stands*). The King is a criminal!

FAIRFAX. Colonel Pride, I have asked you to shut your mouth, sir! Major Harrison, your opinion.

HARRISON. You know it. Bring the King to justice, under the law.

CHILLENDEN. And what is that law?

FAIRFAX (*low*). Indeed.

HARRISON. Make a new law!

GREY. There is no place to bring him to justice.

CHILLENDEN. No. Just cut his head off!

IRETON. The country must see what we do and understand why. There must be a legal process…

GREY. Process, process…

HARRISON. We must be legal...

GREY. There is no court to try a King in!

CHILLENDEN. And no law, only the people's will!

IRETON. Then Parliament will be the court.

HARRISON. Yes! Yes, there we have it.

A pause.

LENTHALL. And if he is found guilty?

HARRISON. Depose him.

GREY. Send him abroad. Or give him a pension, let him pray
out his life as popishly as he likes, in retirement.

CHILLENDEN. Charles Stuart, retired? The people would lay
siege to his hiding place.

PRIDE. Drag him out, beat him to death!

IRETON. No. Find him guilty by *law*. And force him to come
to an agreement.

LILBURNE. The King must be stripped of all powers.
Parliament must be sovereign!

HARRISON. Try him, depose him and declare a republic!

IRETON. Sir, that is unthinkable.

LILBURNE. Not now! (*Points at* HARRISON.) It has just been
thought...

FAIRFAX. Gentlemen, we are all crossways, which-ways here,
we must be of one mind! (*To* CROMWELL.) Oliver...

CROMWELL *shakes his head. He nods to* IRETON.

IRETON. So. God has guided us to send the King to trial.
Trusting that the Almighty will guide His Majesty to come to
a settlement under a new monarchy...

LILBURNE (*on his feet*). We have not agreed that!

PRIDE (*on his feet*). No trial! Have done with the King. Send
God-fearing men to cut his throat!

IRETON. The debate is done. We are decided…

GREY / PRIDE. What? What?

CHILLENDEN. We are not decided! (*To* FAIRFAX.) My Lord?

FAIRFAX. Gentlemen, I…

LILBURNE. Damn you, Ireton, damn you all! I challenge the
lot of you! Fight me! I will duel with you, one after another!

HARRISON (*trying to restrain him*). John…

LILBURNE. You have gone back on what we printed! Oliver,
you agreed! Are you breaking your promise to me? The
people demand what was printed!

CROMWELL. The people demand peace!

A silence.

Harvests planted again and not plundered by the King's
soldiers, or marauding Scots. The family by the hearth, with
no more funerals of husbands and sons killed in civil wars.
In God's name, John: stability, that is the 'will of the people'.

LILBURNE. 'Stability'? Another word for 'tyranny'. You are a
pack of dissembling, juggling knaves!

He tries to attack CROMWELL, *who is impassive. Others
help* HARRISON *restrain him.*

You engineered this, Oliver. So that I'd fall.

CROMWELL. No. You have engineered your own fate. As
Lucifer did.

LILBURNE. Of a sudden you compare me to Satan?

CROMWELL. Yes! You with all your extremists are cast out!

They stare at each other.

Exit all but for CROMWELL, FAIRFAX *and* IRETON.

End of Scene Eight.

Scene Nine

CROMWELL, IRETON, FAIRFAX.

CROMWELL. We will never allow that again.

FAIRFAX. Lilburne's popularity is still great.

IRETON. Challenge it. Arrest him and his preachy, ragbag of followers…

CROMWELL. No.

IRETON. If we don't, we'll have protests, disruptions…

CROMWELL. No. We're all rebels, we have all made each other. But we cut him out. I loved him… but he and his followers never get near this leadership again.

FAIRFAX. They'll still make the Army restless…

CROMWELL. Not if we move quickly and start arrangements for the trial now.

CROMWELL *looks at* FAIRFAX.

FAIRFAX. It has come to that?

CROMWELL. Yes.

FAIRFAX. About the trial. There are questions.

CROMWELL. Such as?

FAIRFAX. Do we have a jury?

CROMWELL. No jury. We will have… (*Invents.*) commissioners. Say: eighty. And we and our followers will sit amongst them.

FAIRFAX *and* IRETON *look at each other. A moment of fear.*

FAIRFAX. We will be the judges?

CROMWELL. With God's help.

Enter a MESSENGER *with a note. Exits.*

IRETON. Oliver, Colonel Hammond is waiting to see us.

CROMWELL. Hammond? Get him.

IRETON *exits.*

We are at one?

FAIRFAX. Yes.

A moment.

Enter IRETON *and* HAMMOND, *who is exhausted. He carries a portfolio. There is mud on his clothes.*

You've been riding hard? Please, Colonel…

HAMMOND *sits.*

HAMMOND. Sirs, you ordered me to intercept any communication His Majesty may attempt.

FAIRFAX. Yes, Colonel…

CROMWELL. Robin, what is the matter?

HAMMOND *takes out a paper.*

HAMMOND. This is a letter that was sent when His Majesty was on the Isle of Wight. It was found on a man in the service of Lord Richmond, attempting to board a ship at Newhaven. A ship bound for Ireland.

A pause. All still.

The letter is to the Duke of Ormonde. It asks him to invade. It is signed by the King.

A pause.

I feel responsible. It was sent when he was in my charge…

CROMWELL. No no, Robin. But speak to no one about this. Please leave us.

HAMMOND *exits.*

IRETON. In the name of God.

CROMWELL. Thomas?

FAIRFAX. I know. It's clear proof of his treason.

And CROMWELL *relaxes. He is amused.*

CROMWELL. Can the King commit treason against himself?

IRETON. The conundrum of our time.

CROMWELL. Do you think Ormonde actually would invade?

FAIRFAX. His effectiveness is overrated. There are factions in his army: old English, new English, Irish papists, Scots Presbyterians. If they got in to boats together I suspect they'd kill each other before they crossed the Irish Sea.

CROMWELL. But that's not the point.

FAIRFAX. No.

CROMWELL. If the King believes there is an army that will rescue him, he will not come to terms. He is subtle.

IRETON. A liar.

CROMWELL. A political man. We may yet get him to behave as a politician.

IRETON. Yes. We move the King again, nearer to London, to Windsor. Let him feel our power. When he is there we will send an emissary. In secret. We will tell him we know of his Irish treachery. He will realise he has to come to terms.

He looks to CROMWELL *for approval.*

CROMWELL (*waves airily*). Whatever is God's will. (*A pause.*) What kind of man is in there?

IRETON. Oliver?

CROMWELL. Within the Royal shell. The hard carapace of ceremony, his claim to a divine right to rule. What man is in there? If I could crack the shell, reach into him. Put my hand in his, pull him to me, our faces close. Then we could speak, low, as human beings, both fallen, both redeemed by the Saviour's blood. And despite all the killing and the horror of these past years, we would settle this. With a prayer. A glass of wine. Even a smile.

IRETON *and* FAIRFAX *are shocked. Then they laugh.*

What?

FAIRFAX. The thought of you and Charles Stuart raising a glass.

IRETON. The world turned inside out.

FAIRFAX. Riots in the streets.

IRETON. All disorientated.

CROMWELL (*not amused*). This is a world disorientated! We swing we know not where or which way. We must right ourselves. Or the country and all of us will go to Hell.

End of Scene Nine.

Scene Ten

FAIRFAX *and* IRETON *leave the stage.* CROMWELL *alone.*

Enter LENTHALL.

CROMWELL. Speaker Lenthall.

LENTHALL. Lieutenant General.

CROMWELL. The Army leadership has a delicate and important task for you.

LENTHALL. I am pleased to serve.

CROMWELL. The King is to be moved to Windsor. You are to go to him there, secretly. Secretly! And offer him certain terms.

LENTHALL. Yes, General.

CROMWELL. You will also give him a personal message from me. None of this will be on paper. (*A moment.*) You will tell His Majesty that if he settles with the Army, even now, there need not be a trial.

LENTHALL. I...

CROMWELL. Tell him that.

LENTHALL. I cannot speak for Parliament...

CROMWELL. No, you will be speaking for me.

A pause.

LENTHALL. Yes, General.

LENTHALL *exits.*

CROMWELL. Lord, is Your power in my hand? Do I still hold Your sword, to make peace?

Exit CROMWELL.

End of Scene Ten.

Scene Eleven

Windsor Castle. Room. Firelight. CHARLES *alone. He has been and is drinking wine.*

CHARLES. Henrietta.

Enter HAMMOND. *He waits to be spoken to.*

Ah, my gaoler. Now my only courtier. I do hope they treat Richmond with decency. Do you have any word of him?

HAMMOND. No, Sire, but...

CHARLES. No. News out of the Tower of London is rare. Such walls. Such silence. Such fear. (*Laughs.*) To think of Cromwell and his Devil's crew, now imprisoning dukes in the Tower! Up and round, up and round, rise and tumble...

HAMMOND. There is an emissary.

CHARLES. Oh, an emissary!

HAMMOND. With a message from the Army Council.

CHARLES. I never went to mass with the Queen.

HAMMOND. I...

CHARLES. Queen Henrietta had her own Roman priest, her own private chapels at Whitehall Palace, Richmond, here at Windsor. But I never joined her. She worshipped alone.

HAMMOND. Your M…

CHARLES. My Parliamentary enemies would so love to believe I did worship with her. Secret popery in the palaces. The King on his knees in the deep of night, a Catholic wafer on his tongue.

HAMMOND. Your Majesty…

CHARLES. But you see…

HAMMOND *irritated.*

No no, I want you to understand the point. I believe the Church of England is the true Church. It is the papal throne that is heretical, not mine. Anglicanism is the true, Catholic religion. A Church that is a thousand years old. What a comfort religion can be. To caress the mind with a little theology.

HAMMOND. Your Majesty, the emissary.

CHARLES. Oh yes. (*A giggle*.) Emitted from where? Where do they come from, these people? These men with serious eyes before burning, rebel brains. Where do they spawn? Are there nests of them, like wasps, in the dark corners of my Kingdom, sewer backstreets where no king's man goes? These people, these people… Puritans! Why do they wear black hats?

HAMMOND. You must see him.

CHARLES. No.

HAMMOND. He has been sent personally, in secrecy, by Lieutenant General Cromwell.

CHARLES. Cromwell. Everywhere that name, everywhere that hand. Moving things. Even a king, castle to castle, at a whim. Is he a man at all? Or just a force.

HAMMOND. He is a man.

CHARLES. Oh, in shape, form, no doubt, a man: head, a hangable neck, like all of you.

HAMMOND *tries to intervene again*.

But I wonder. I sense something within him. Something... molten. Hot. Like lead, when over a fire, liquid, silvery, splashing, burning...

HAMMOND....

CHARLES. Or is he just dull, cold metal? The dullness within of a Huntingdon farmer. A fenland flatness, a mind of ditches and gripes. If we did meet, perhaps he would be, after all, small. And kneel. And we would put all the blood behind us, king and subject. And be at peace.

HAMMOND. Your Majesty, I beg you.

CHARLES. I will not see his messenger.

HAMMOND. Your Majesty just spoke of peace?

CHARLES. Did I?

HAMMOND. You cannot refuse.

CHARLES. What did you say?

HAMMOND. You cannot refuse!

CHARLES. Ah, Robin. You have always shown me the greatest courtesy. Are you about to withdraw it?

HAMMOND. I should drag you down in chains to see this man.

CHARLES. Then do so.

A pause.

HAMMOND. I beg you.

CHARLES. You beg? Oh, I have waited so long for rebels to beg. At least now one has!

HAMMOND. Your Majesty would be so well advised to...

CHARLES. All the advice I need I have from Heaven!

A pause.

HAMMOND. What shall I tell the…

CHARLES. Tell him he is another torso for the executioner! Another head for a pike! Tell him to go to Hell.

He drinks.

End of Scene Eleven.

Scene Twelve

Enter CROMWELL, IRETON, FAIRFAX *and* LENTHALL.

IRETON. Would not see you?

LENTHALL. No.

IRETON. You insisted…

LENTHALL. Repeatedly.

FAIRFAX. And Hammond?

LENTHALL. He did all he could.

IRETON. And you were there all day…

LENTHALL. Until the King went to bed.

IRETON. To bed!

CROMWELL. So… you were able to give the King no message at all?

LENTHALL. No, General.

CROMWELL. No part of it.

LENTHALL. No.

CROMWELL. And he knew I had sent you. Personally.

LENTHALL. I am sure of it.

A pause. They are all looking at CROMWELL.

CROMWELL. Until now… in my conscience… I turned and twisted, this way, that way. In prayer, in hope, but in darkness. But now, suddenly, there is clear light. Now I hear the voice of providence, loud and clear. The King must stand trial. And if needs must… (*A moment.*) I tell you, we will cut off his head! Cut it off! Cut it off! With the crown upon it!

End of Act One.

ACT TWO

Scene One

JOHN COOKE *and* MARY COOKE*'s home.*

JOHN *alone. A Bible on a stand. He takes the Bible, opens it and points at a passage at random.*

COOKE (*reads, Psalm 39 v9*). 'I was dumb. I opened not my mouth.' Why am I dumb? For what should I open my mouth? Lord, help me. (*Opens the Bible again and points at random. Reads. Numbers 14 v29.*) 'The Amalekites dwell in the land of the South: and the Hittites, and the Jebusites, and the Amorites, dwell in the mountains: and the Canaanites dwell by the sea, and by the coast of Jordan.' (*Closes the Bible, bewildered.*) Lord?

Enter MARY.

MARY. John.

COOKE. What?

MARY. Oh, John.

COOKE. Mary my love, what is the matter?

MARY. It's...

COOKE. Is the boy ill?

MARY. No. It's the. In person. Himself.

COOKE. Who?

MARY. Lieutenant General Cromwell.

They stare at each other, stunned.

COOKE. Here?

MARY. Yes. John, what does he want?

COOKE. How can I know till I've spoken to him?

MARY. Lawyers! Always so logical.

COOKE. Mary…

MARY. He's not going to arrest you, is he? For your past? And mine? With the radicals?

COOKE. If I were to be arrested in the middle of the night, I don't think General Cromwell would come to do it personally.

MARY. If you must drink a bitter cup, I will drink it with you.

COOKE. I fear this cup will be bitter.

MARY. You know what he wants?

COOKE. Bring him in, Mary.

A moment.

She exits.

'I was dumb. I opened not my…'

Enter MARY, CROMWELL *and, at a discreet distance,* BRADSHAW.

CROMWELL. Master Cooke, Mrs Cooke, forgive the late hour. You have a little son I think…

MARY. Ezekiel.

CROMWELL. Ezekiel, yes, I hope he is well?

MARY. He is very well, General.

CROMWELL. I pray to God he may grow to be a man in a better England.

MARY. Which with God's help we must make.

CROMWELL. Indeed.

A difficult moment. The men want her to leave, she does not.

COOKE. Mary, perhaps some wine for the Lieutenant General…

CROMWELL (*smiles*). Oh, I was told you refused alcohol.

MARY. Told?

CROMWELL. I have enquired.

A touch of fear.

COOKE. We do not partake, but it would be rude to deny our guests.

CROMWELL. You are temperate.

MARY. Strictly so. But for lapses.

CROMWELL (*smiles*). So you are temperately temperate.

But that is lost on them. And MARY *gives in.*

MARY. Call me if you need food or. Bread and cheese or. Water or. Yes.

She exits but sneaks back on to overhear.

CROMWELL. Master Cooke.

COOKE. General.

CROMWELL *is judging the moment.*

CROMWELL. You once defended John Lilburne in the law courts.

COOKE. Yes.

CROMWELL. When the King still had power over the law. And life and death.

COOKE. Yes.

CROMWELL. You argued for the defendant's right of silence.

COOKE. Yes.

CROMWELL. You have a reputation for courage, for taking difficult cases.

COOKE. I do my duty as the Lord tells me.

CROMWELL. You are aware that Parliament has set up a High Court to try His Majesty the King.

COOKE. Who in this land could not be aware the King is to be tried for his life?

CROMWELL. Indeed. The High Court wishes to appoint you as Solicitor General.

A moment.

COOKE. Solicitor…

CROMWELL. You will be the Chief Prosecutor.

MARY. Oh. Oh. Saints. Saints arrayed in rows, oh.

COOKE. Sir, there are many other lawyers far more qualified than I am…

CROMWELL. Undoubtedly, but they have all mysteriously left London. And in midwinter. I wonder why that is? There is no danger of plague in this cold weather. But I tell you, John Cooke, perhaps lawyers fleeing the capital for fear of this task is a winnowing by the Lord. He who remains is honest. You remain.

MARY (*overhearing*). But why must it be you? Always you, always the good John. The cut stalk on the threshing floor, to be beaten, to be chaff. That's my John.

CROMWELL. Do you have the courage to do this?

MARY. Yes you do, my love. You silly fool. Say no. No, yes, no.

COOKE. I will not be dumb. I will open my mouth. (*To* CROMWELL.) With God's help, yes, I will do it.

MARY *turns away.* CROMWELL *and* COOKE *grip each other by the forearms, ecstatic.*

CROMWELL. This is John Bradshaw.

BRADSHAW. Mr Cooke.

COOKE. Sir.

CROMWELL. He is Chief Justice in Chester.

COOKE. I know your reputation, sir. You once defended John Milton in Chancery.

BRADSHAW. I did.

COOKE. A godly man.

BRADSHAW. Indeed. Though with a high opinion of his verses.

CROMWELL. Mr Bradshaw will be President of the Court.

BRADSHAW. Another lowly lawyer called to great heights.

COOKE. Yes.

CROMWELL. Gentlemen! This is our comfort: God is in Heaven.

COOKE. God is in Heaven.

BRADSHAW. God is in Heaven.

CROMWELL. God is in Heaven and He does what pleases Him.

COOKE. Yes, His and only His counsel shall stand.

CROMWELL. His counsel shall stand!

BRADSHAW. It shall stand!

COOKE. It shall stand!

CROMWELL. His counsel shall stand, whatever the designs of evil men and the fury of tyrants. Amen.

COOKE. Amen.

BRADSHAW. Amen.

They embrace.

MARY. Amen to. Life. Amen, our life. Goodbye, life. Amen.

End of Scene One.

Scene Two

LORD FAIRFAX*'s house*.

FAIRFAX *alone for a moment*.

Enter CROMWELL, *in haste,* ANNE *following*.

CROMWELL. Bradshaw has agreed to be President of the Court.

FAIRFAX. Bradshaw? Do I know him?

CROMWELL. He is Chief Justice in the Sherriff's Court at Chester.

FAIRFAX. Chester?

CROMWELL. He has a good reputation.

FAIRFAX. You mean more senior judges refused.

CROMWELL. Bradshaw is good.

FAIRFAX. Who for Solicitor General?

CROMWELL. John Cooke.

ANNE. Not the…

CROMWELL. Yes! The radical who defended John Lilburne.

ANNE. And you are to try His Majesty for his life with these Puritan dregs?

CROMWELL. They are brave men.

ANNE. They are low men.

CROMWELL. And how 'high' must we be, then, to say 'no' to a king?

ANNE. Only one is high enough. And He is in Heaven.

CROMWELL. Indeed. And we are doing His work upon Earth.

ANNE. You really believe that?

CROMWELL. What else can I believe, Lady Anne? What choice do I have but to believe that?

ANNE. Sir, do not raise your voice in my house!

FAIRFAX. Anne, please leave us.

ANNE. No I will not.

FAIRFAX. Madam!

ANNE. Thomas, tell him.

A pause.

CROMWELL. Well? Tell me what?

FAIRFAX. I will not serve as a commissioner at the trial.

A pause.

I will not be a juror judging the King.

CROMWELL. But you are Commander of the Army. There is no question. You must be a commissioner.

FAIRFAX. No.

CROMWELL. Thomas, all we have done…

ANNE. You are not to dissuade him…

CROMWELL. …All we have experienced…

ANNE (*to* FAIRFAX). …Do not listen…

CROMWELL. …All we prayed for, through all the fights, the terrible losses – Edgehill, the streams of wounded down to Kineton Village – and the triumphs, Naseby, Prince Rupert's cavalry defeated and the King running away, leaving his banner in the mud – all that comes to this moment. Now. When we can remake England for ever.

FAIRFAX. I cannot do it.

CROMWELL. 'Cannot'?

FAIRFAX. I have kept up a charade. For the sake of unity in the Army. For the sake of our comradeship, Oliver. But I cannot sit in judgement of the King.

CROMWELL. Then don't.

FAIRFAX. I had a letter from the Queen herself in Holland, begging me... I am torn.

CROMWELL. Then tear. The country is ripped to bits, why should we not be? You will not serve?

FAIRFAX *shakes his head.*

(*Making to leave.*) I have work.

FAIRFAX. To think you and I have come to this.

CROMWELL. Well, we have.

They look at each other.

Goodnight to you. (*Nods to* ANNE.) My Lady.

He exits quickly.

ANNE. You're Commander-in-Chief! Go to the Council and order them to stop the trial.

FAIRFAX. That would be stony ground.

ANNE. Then split the Army. Raise a force against Cromwell, Ireton and the Council. They launched a coup against the Presbyterians, launch a coup against them. Save the King.

FAIRFAX. No! No. I am out of it. I will resign my commission.

ANNE. You cannot! Do that and you know what will happen.

FAIRFAX. Perhaps God's will?

ANNE. God cannot will the King's death. How can He? (*Low.*) Charles Stuart is the Lord's anointed.

FAIRFAX. Be quiet now. Be quiet. It is so cold. Why won't it snow? If there were snow over everything, white, pure... snow. Then maybe we'd have... peace.

He stops. She touches his face.

ANNE. Oh, Thomas. You are so tired.

End of Scene Two.

Scene Three

Westminster Hall. State pomp.

COMMISSIONERS – *i.e. the jury – on tiers of benches.*
CROMWELL *and* IRETON *sit on a bench downstage, also*
HARRISON, LENTHALL *and* HAMMOND. SOLDIERS,
behind them SPECTATORS. *A gallery.* ANNE *sits in it, high
above the scene.*

*An imposing chair and a table on a dais. On the table is a
crimson cushion with the mace and sword – the symbols of
Parliament – resting on it.*

A large armchair, covered in red velvet, waits for the King.

COOKE *sits at a small table, shuffling papers.*

IRETON *looks up and sees* ANNE.

IRETON. Lady Fairfax.

> CROMWELL *looks up. He and* ANNE *catch each other's
> eye.*

No sign of her husband.

CROMWELL. That is for his conscience.

IRETON. In the name of all the Saints, Oliver, the Commander
of the Army must be here…

CROMWELL. He will be, he will not. Be blithe, Henry. Dice
are thrown, we all tumble, to come face up or not.

IRETON. The wife could be disruptive. I'll have her removed…

CROMWELL. No no.

FIRST VOICE. All stand for the President of the Court!

SECOND VOICE. All stand for the President of the Court!

> BRADSHAW *enters. He wears red robes.*
>
> *He sits. All sit.*

BRADSHAW. Bring the prisoner into the court.

Enter CHARLES. *He is dressed entirely in black but for a white-lace collar. Around his neck there is the blue ribbon and jewelled emblem of St George. On his black cloak there is the large silver star of the Order of the Garter. He carries a black cane with a silver knob.*

Two TROOPERS, *fully armed, accompany him.*

No one stands. CHARLES *waits for a moment.*

CHARLES (*low, without moving his head*). Which one is Master Cromwell?

FIRST TROOPER (*very nervous*). End of the lower bench. Your Majesty.

CHARLES *gives no sign of having heard him. He stands still a little longer, then makes his way to the chair and sits.*

BRADSHAW. Charles Stuart, King of England, the Commons of England assembled in Parliament, deeply aware of the calamities you have brought upon this nation, have resolved to bring you to trial and judgement. For that purpose, they have constituted this High Court of Justice, before which you are brought.

CHARLES *looks directly at* CROMWELL.

CROMWELL *raises his head and looks back.*

CHARLES *looks away.*

Mr Cooke. Please read the charge against the prisoner.

COOKE *stands.*

COOKE. I am commanded to charge Charles Stuart, King of England…

CHARLES *taps* COOKE *on the shoulder with his cane.*

CHARLES. Hold, sir.

A gasp in the court.

COOKE. I am commanded to charge…

Again, CHARLES *taps his shoulder.*

CHARLES. Hold, sir.

COOKE....charge...

CHARLES (*taps again*). Hold, sir.

The knob of the cane falls off. It rolls on the floor and stops.

Everyone looks at it, no one moves.

CHARLES *stands and walks slowly to the knob of the cane, bends and picks it up.*

Another gasp in the court.

CHARLES *looks about with disdain and returns to his seat.*

CROMWELL. I did not know the man was a play actor.

IRETON. We closed the theatres, we will close him.

CROMWELL *is not amused.*

BRADSHAW. Mr Solicitor for the Commonwealth, please continue.

ANNE. Where is Lord Fairfax? Where is the Commander of the Army?

MAN'S VOICE. Hold your tongue, woman!

ANNE. I tell you all, my husband would not sit in this court! Ever!

BRADSHAW. No one further is to call out.

ANNE. Oliver Cromwell is a traitor!

BRADSHAW. No one!

ANNE *pushes her way out of the gallery and exits.*

The Court settles.

COOKE. I am commanded to charge Charles Stuart, King of England, in the name of the Commons of England, with treason.

CHARLES *laughs, loudly.*

COOKE *unrolls a parchment. He reads, though he has committed the charges to memory.*

There are six counts to the charge. One: as King of England you had a wicked design to give yourself unlimited and tyrannical power, to overthrow the rights and liberties of the people. Two: with your tyrannical power, you traitorously went to war against Parliament and the people it represents. Three: you launched many terrible battles, losing the lives of thousands – Edge Hill, Bristol, Marston Moor, Newbury, Naseby and many other murderous fights. Four: you entreated foreign states to invade this country. Five: last year you caused a second civil war, for the sake of your personal power and against the common right, liberty, justice and peace of the people of this nation. Six: even now you are conspiring with Catholic forces in Ireland to launch a third civil war. In conclusion: you, Charles Stuart, are responsible for all the treasons, murders, rapes, burnings, spoils, desolations, damages and mischiefs to this nation, acted in these wars. You are a tyrant, a traitor and a murderer, a public and implacable enemy of the Commonwealth of England.

A rumbling sound from the crowd.

BRADSHAW. You have now heard the charge. The Court expects your answer.

All fall silent and are still.

CHARLES. I would know by what power I am called here. I would know by what authority, I mean *lawful* authority. There are many unlawful authorities in the world: thieves and robbers by the highways. I was recently in the Isle of Wight. I would know by what authority I am brought from there, and carried from place to place, and I know not what. When I know by what lawful authority this is done, I shall answer.

COOKE *is about to speak but* CHARLES *interrupts him.*

Remember I am your King, your lawful King, and what sins you bring on your heads, and the judgement of God upon this land. Think upon it, I say, think well upon it, before you go from one sin to a greater. Therefore, let me know by what lawful authority I am seated here.

COOKE *looks lost.*

BRADSHAW. You are brought here in the name of the people of England, of whom you are elected King, to answer to them.

CHARLES. 'Elected'? England was never an elective kingdom. It is an hereditary kingdom and has been for a thousand years. I do stand more for the liberty of my people than any here that come to be my pretended judges. Therefore, let me know by what lawful authority I am seated here and I will answer.

COOKE. Sir, if you do not acknowledge the Court, constituted lawfully by the House of Commons, we may have to proceed nevertheless.

CHARLES (*turns on* COOKE). Sir! I will stand for the privilege of the House of Commons as much as any man here. But is this the coming of a king freely to his parliament? No, sir! Is, then, my being dragged here an end of the treaty of public faith between people and king? Let me see a legal authority warranted by the word of God, the Scriptures, or the constitution of the kingdom.

CROMWELL (*low*). Stop it, Bradshaw, stop the thing now.

BRADSHAW. Sir. Seeing you will not answer, the Court will adjourn to consider.

CHARLES. There is a God in Heaven, that will call you, and all that give you power, to account.

BRADSHAW. Sir, we are adjourned to Monday next. Then you will answer.

CHARLES. You have shown no lawful authority!

COOKE. Our authority is God's and that of the Kingdom.

CHARLES. God has entrusted me to keep the peace of this realm, not you.

COOKE. The peace you speak of will be kept in the doing of justice, and that is our present work.

BRADSHAW. In the meantime, those that brought you here are to take you back again.

Everyone stands, but for CHARLES.

A silence, all waiting.

Then CHARLES *stands. He points at the sword on the table.*

CHARLES. I do not fear that.

He walks away slowly, the two TROOPERS *behind him, and exits.*

VOICE. God save the King!

OTHER VOICES. Justice, justice!

Pushing and shoving and scuffles.

End of Scene Three.

Scene Four

CROMWELL, HARRISON, IRETON, LENTHALL, HAMMOND, COOKE *and* BRADSHAW, *mid-argument.*

CROMWELL – *typically biding his time – lurks on the edge of the group.*

HARRISON. We have to!

LENTHALL. We cannot.

HARRISON. Allow the King to continue like this and we are lost.

IRETON. There is great danger here.

HARRISON. Yes. The public have never heard his voice before. Now they find he speaks like an angel.

IRETON. I say, exclude the public. Continue the trial in secret.

HARRISON. I agree.

COOKE (*to* IRETON). General, forgive me, but do that and what would we look like to the world?

LENTHALL. He's right. Justice must be seen to be done.

BRADSHAW. But the public could riot, if the King stirs them! We have had shouts for the King.

LENTHALL. And for justice.

BRADSHAW. Then Lady Fairfax crying out! What if there are more high-born protests?

HARRISON. Set an example. Arrest her.

CROMWELL. Leave her be.

HARRISON. But…

CROMWELL. I said leave her be!

CROMWELL *turns away.*

A pause.

BRADSHAW. Very well, as President of the Court I suggest that the trial continues in public, but I announce that anyone crying out will be arrested and imprisoned.

LENTHALL. Yes.

COOKE. Yes.

HARRISON. Yes.

IRETON *nods.*

Nothing from CROMWELL.

IRETON. Gentlemen, to the heart of our problem. We have been ambushed. The King's sense of law is better than we thought. Also his power of expression.

BRADSHAW. Absolutely! That with the cane, did he arrange that?

LENTHALL. You mean he loosened the knob himself…

HAMMOND. No no, that was chance.

HARRISON. Hammond, you have guarded him all these months. Do you expect this public display from him?

HAMMOND. No. I always thought him one for weasel words, in private.

IRETON. What I have to ask, despite his power of speech…
What I have to ask, in complete secrecy, is this. (*Turns to the two lawyers.*) How good is his case?

A pause.

COOKE. We sail in uncharted waters.

BRADSHAW. Yes. What we are doing is unprecedented. Kings have been deposed before, but in factional fights, like in the time of Richard III. Brute force has removed tyrannical kings, but never law.

HARRISON. What the King has done is unprecedented! And so should be our response.

IRETON. Yes! Make new law!

COOKE. With respect, no. We must be just, we must act within the established common law.

LENTHALL. True, if we don't, even though we cut off his head, he'll have won. The execution would be seen as unlawful.

A pause.

HARRISON. We could simply go ahead without a plea from the King?

BRADSHAW. That is against the first principle of justice. Prisoners must plead guilty or not guilty!

IRETON. Why doesn't he just say: 'not guilty'?

COOKE. Because then, General, he would have acknowledged the Court to be legal!

CROMWELL. We must continue as we have begun.

They all look at CROMWELL.

Charles Stuart will show his contempt for the English people. The King will condemn himself.

IRETON. Let us pray so. But we must rein him in.

CROMWELL (*to* BRADSHAW). Tell the prisoner that any further protests from him and the Court will enter a guilty plea. And we will have only two more sessions, Monday and Tuesday afternoons. That means the execution will be on Saturday.

COOKE. Should he be found guilty.

They all look at him.

A pause.

IRETON. Major Harrison, please tell our fellow commissioners what is going to happen. I am sure they will agree.

HARRISON. Yes, General.

HARRISON *exits.*

CROMWELL. Gentlemen.

COOKE, BRADSHAW, HAMMOND *and* LENTHALL *exit.*

IRETON. So. We are going to execute him.

CROMWELL. Is his head still on his shoulders?

IRETON. What's your meaning?

CROMWELL. My meaning is… his head still sits amid that exquisite collar, Antwerp lace I believe, starched, my mother always speaks wistfully of Antwerp lace…

He stops.

IRETON. Well, you could send to Antwerp…

CROMWELL. No no, you don't understand, she makes it herself. Needle and bobbin. The flowerpot design. Those strong hands, farmer's wife's hands, picking at the thread. Last time I was home, that's what she did. In silence. Disapproving silence.

IRETON. Mrs Cromwell disapproves of the trial?

CROMWELL. No, she disapproves of the King still being alive.

IRETON. Ah.

CROMWELL *laughs.*

CROMWELL. The force of purity, Henry.

IRETON. It is dangerous.

CROMWELL. Yes. But it has its beauty. We will get there in
the end. Find him guilty, within the law. Shock him… and at
last he will change, and settle.

IRETON. Can you believe that? Even now?

CROMWELL. We wait upon the Lord.

IRETON. And you hear His voice in this.

A pause.

Oliver? You hear the Lord's voice?

CROMWELL *turns away without replying.*

End of Scene Four.

Scene Five

JOHN *and* MARY COOKE*'s home.*

MARY. No king! No king! It will be a wondrous thing. I must
come to the trial.

COOKE. I've told you, Mary, I don't want you there.

MARY. Why? It's joyous!

COOKE. No it's not. Not joyous at all.

MARY. I want to be there. In the light of the glory of what we
do at the King's trial.

COOKE. No! You must… keep a distance.

MARY. When have I kept distances, ever?

COOKE. I don't want you there because… it may go wrong.

MARY. How could it 'go wrong', silly?

COOKE. By the people turning against us? By the case falling apart legally? For it is not secure. And by... by the King raising a troop of friends and storming Westminster Hall? By us all getting hanged and quartered at Tyburn?

MARY. I dreaded you being Prosecutor. But now I'm glad. Should I not be?

He is about to reply but there is an urgent knock at the door. For a moment they are afraid.

MARY *goes to answer.*

JOHN. No, stay.

He exits.

MARY *looks at the Bible on its stand. She opens it and points at a passage.*

MARY (*reads, Job 5 v1*). 'Call now, if there will be any that will answer thee; and to which of the Saints wilt thou turn?'

Enter COOKE *with* LILBURNE.

Free John. Tell my husband to let me go to the trial on Monday.

LILBURNE. Why should you wish to go there, Mary?

MARY. To see a new England born, John.

LILBURNE. Ha! Stillborn.

MARY. No no, aren't you joyful that England is to have no king?

LILBURNE. No king, but what in his place? The Army Council, under the heel of Cromwell and Ireton.

COOKE. But the power of monarchy is broken.

LILBURNE. But the power of Parliament is broken.

COOKE. Cromwell will restore it.

LILBURNE. I think not.

MARY. If you are not for what they will do on Monday, why are you here?

LILBURNE. John. Refuse to continue with the prosecution.

A pause.

COOKE. You know I cannot do that.

LILBURNE. Cromwell uses you, John, your honesty, your good faith. You are the innocent mask to his dictatorial ways.

COOKE. You don't understand him.

LILBURNE. The Court was set up by a purged Parliament.

COOKE. It is the best we can do!

LILBURNE. The best you can do?

COOKE. It is imperfect. We invent as we go along. But the Lord's work must be done.

LILBURNE. 'The Lord's work', you begin to sound like Oliver...

MARY. It is the Lord's work. And when England is free from the tyranny of royalty, we will build a free Parliament.

LILBURNE. John, come the spring, the Levellers are resolved to move against the Council.

MARY. More fighting...

COOKE. That will divide the Army...

LILBURNE. We still have massive support. We will send agitators out, unite the radicals in the Army. If we do not, Cromwell will purge the Army of all Levellers.

COOKE. Perhaps he will be right to do so.

A silence.

LILBURNE. You really are his creature now.

COOKE. There is no choice, John. The King must be felled with what we have to hand. Now.

LILBURNE. You sadden me. I thought you dreamt with us of a better world.

COOKE. Dreams achieve nothing. We must wake and do as best we can.

LILBURNE. You saved my life in court, once. Now you destroy it. Goodbye, John, goodbye, Mary.

He exits.

MARY. 'To which of the Saints wilt thou turn?' And we turn to Oliver.

COOKE. No Saints. Only sinners.

He is distressed.

MARY. Well, maybe we can sin to the good. Sin to the good.

COOKE *smiles.*

COOKE. Yes.

He embraces her.

End of Scene Five.

Scene Six

The Court reassembles. A hum of conversation, people turned to each other. It continues as CHARLES *enters and takes his place.*

COOKE *is having a conversation with* LENTHALL, *they are looking at a paper* COOKE *holds.*

CHARLES *pokes* COOKE *in the back with his cane.*

CHARLES. Sir, sir, come on!

COOKE *wheels round in a fury. All are suddenly silent.* CHARLES *stares at* COOKE.

COOKE (*to* BRADSHAW). May it please Your Lordship, Lord President. I did at the last session, on behalf of the Commons of England, exhibit and give in to this Court a charge of high treason against the prisoner at the bar. He was not then pleased to give an answer but disputed the authority of this

High Court. My motion to the Court, on behalf of the Kingdom of England, is that the prisoner be directed to make a positive answer: guilty, yes or no.

BRADSHAW (*to* CHARLES). Sir, you heard a charge read out against you of high treason. You were pleased to reply that you did not know by what authority you were brought here. You were given the answer: that it is by the authority of the Commons of England assembled in Parliament. It is the people of the Kingdom of England that call you to account. Therefore, confess to the charge or deny it. You are to lose no more time and give a positive answer.

A silence.

CHARLES. A king cannot be tried by any superior jurisdiction on Earth...

BRADSHAW. Sir, I must interrupt you. You are about to enter into argument again concerning the authority of this Court. You may not do that. You are a prisoner and charged as a high delinquent.

CHARLES. I do not know how a king can be a delinquent. The Crown is the sole authority in English courts. Can I arrest myself?

Someone in the gallery laughs. Heads turn.

BRADSHAW. Sir, do not attack the jurisdiction of this Court! We sit here by the authority of the Commons of England. All your predecessors, and you, are responsible to them.

CHARLES. I deny that. Show me one precedent.

BRADSHAW. Sir, do not interrupt while the Court is speaking to you!

CHARLES. I am no lawyer, for which, perhaps, I should thank the Almighty...

Again someone laughs.

But I say, sir, by your favour, that the House of Commons is not and never was a court of judicature.

IRETON (*low to* CROMWELL). He has found a crack.

CHARLES. I require you to tell me: how is the House of Commons a court?

BRADSHAW. It is not for prisoners to require.

CHARLES. Sir, I am not an ordinary prisoner!

Cries begin and grow from the public as the exchange gets out of hand: 'Justice!'/ 'The King!'

BRADSHAW. The Court has considered.

CHARLES. You never heard my reasons yet.

BRADSHAW. Sir, your reasons are not to be heard against the higher jurisdiction…

CHARLES. Show me a jurisdiction, any court that can be called just, in which reason is not to be heard…

COOKE. Sir, we show it to you here, the Commons of England!

CHARLES. What? No reason here?

COOKE. I did not mean…

BRADSHAW. Take away the prisoner…

But the TROOPERS *hesitate.*

CHARLES. It is the King not you who protects the liberty and freedom of all his subjects…

COOKE. Sir, how great a friend or not you have been to the liberty of the people, against whom you took up arms, let all England and the world judge!

CHARLES. Sir, under favour… I never took up arms against the laws!

BRADSHAW. The command of the Court must be obeyed: no answer will be given to the charge.

CHARLES. Well, sir! Well!

CHARLES and the Court disperse and exit.

End of Scene Six.

Scene Seven

CROMWELL, HARRISON, IRETON, LENTHALL, COOKE
and BRADSHAW.

CROMWELL. You lawyers had best explain yourselves, and in
words a plain man and the Good Lord above can understand!

BRADSHAW. The House of Commons is not a judicature.

CROMWELL. What, in the bowels of Christ, is that!

BRADSHAW. A judicature is a body that has the power of
dispensing justice by legal power.

COOKE. Actually... actually... There is nothing in history that
says the Commons *can* order a trial.

BRADSHAW. He's right. The Commons is not an assizes, it is
not a court of law.

CROMWELL. Then we will make it one.

HARRISON. How can we do that?

CROMWELL. By Act of Parliament. Now. In the morning.

IRETON. Yes.

BRADSHAW. There is a technical procedure. The House can
pass an ordinance. The trial can then be in Chancery, yes, Mr
Cooke?

COOKE. Technically, yes, though...

CROMWELL. I care not by what quaint device, but establish
the legality of the Court. Now!

HAMMOND. What grounds are we treading on here...?

CROMWELL. The future ground of England, sir. We will make
Parliament the most powerful thing in the land. So no King
can ever again claim to be mightier than the will of the
people. We are not just trying a tyrant, we are inventing a
country. We are in an unknown region, floating on nothing,

trying to think thoughts never thought before; we are in mid-air, Heaven above us, Hell beneath. There is but one thing sustains us from falling to utter ruin: that the Lord God Almighty's purpose is to make His people free, as He did when the Israelites fled from Egypt and the tyranny of the Pharaoh. Well! We have *our* Pharaoh. But we cannot flee, we are already in our promised land, our dear, suffering, torn and bleeding but still beautiful England. So what will God have us do? For what has He given us victory after victory? Why, it is clear: to take Pharaoh's power from him and give it to God's children. And we will do that. And in days to come, people will say it is the best thing in the world to be a citizen of England, because of England's Parliament. So! So! Only one more day of games with Charles Stuart. If he will not enter a plea, find him guilty and condemn him.

HAMMOND. I cannot agree to this.

CROMWELL. Robin, listen to me, I know your decency, your feelings for the King as a man, through these difficult days. But we must not fall into disunion amongst ourselves. I am confident we are doing our duty and waiting upon the Lord. We shall find He will be as a wall of brass round us, until we have finished this work.

HAMMOND. I pray so, Oliver.

CROMWELL. Good. Gentlemen! Much to do! The drafting of Parliamentary ordinances, the phrasings of Court speeches, all the gobble-di hobble-di comings and goings of tomorrow! Go to work and God be with you!

OTHERS. God be with you, General / God be with you, Oliver / God be with you.

Exit all but for CROMWELL.

He paces back and forth. He takes out a Bible. He holds it to his chest, head bowed, eyes closed. He opens his eyes and holds the Bible out.

A pause.

He opens the Bible quickly, at random. He is about to point but cannot.

CROMWELL (*reads, Numbers 13 v18*). 'And what the land is that they dwell in.' (*Snaps the Bible shut.*) Yes, what is the land we live in? What is it to be? Kingdom? Republic, like in Roman times? Democracy, like some lunatics in the Army dream of, all things held in common? What is the land?

He opens the Bible again and points.

(*Reads, II Kings 19 v24.*) 'I have digged and drunk strange waters, and with the sole of my feet have I dried up the rivers of besieged places.' (*Snaps the Bible shut.*) Strange waters indeed, drunk from ditches on battlefields. Besieged cities. Gloucester, in '43, the King's Army at the gates. A month of bombardments, the suffering, the stench, the cries of the wounded in the streets. But Parliament sent an army, the siege was lifted. The King's Army withdrew. But you remind me now, oh Lord, of the cost.

He opens the Bible again and points.

(*Reads, Matthew 5.9.*) 'Blessed are the peacemakers, for they shall be called the children of God.'

The Bible is still open in his hands. He pauses, his head bowed. Then he slowly closes the Bible and exits.

End of Scene Seven.

Scene Eight

Sir Robert Cotton's house – where CHARLES *is being held. He is seated at a table, reading law books. There is wine in a decanter and glasses.*

CROMWELL *enters behind him.*

CHARLES. Good evening to you, Master Cromwell.

CROMWELL. Your Majesty. I wish to be civil.

CHARLES. Civil. (*A moment.*) I have good manners left to me, though little else. Will you take some wine?

CROMWELL. Thank you.

> CHARLES *gestures to the table.* CROMWELL *sits.* CHARLES *pours him a glass of wine.*

CHARLES. You don't condemn wine, like some of your co-religionists?

CROMWELL. True, there are some in Parliament who would keep all the wine out of the country, for the fear that some will get drunk. Extremes of opinion bring many errors.

CHARLES. Indeed.

> *They drink, but not much, and put the glasses down on the table at the same time. The glasses remain untouched until the end of the scene.*

> *A long silence.*

CROMWELL. It is appalling cold weather.

CHARLES. Yes. I have taken to wearing three shirts.

CROMWELL. I hope there are coals enough for the fire here…

CHARLES. Yes yes. Three shirts, not to shiver when I stand before the block. Let alone sneeze. That would make a bad impression.

CROMWELL. Sire, you need not stand there.

CHARLES. What? No need? After all the abuse of Parliament, the wrecking of my Kingdom, the imprisonment of my person, this trial, suddenly, no need? Well well.

CROMWELL. We are two men in a room. Here we sit, the firelight on both of us. You with your fear of cold, I with my sore head. Can we come to understand each other?

A moment.

CHARLES. My father. (*A moment.*) My father, the late King, used to visit your uncle, Sir Oliver.

CROMWELL. Yes, at Hinchingbrooke. For hunting.

CHARLES. My father felt warmly toward your family.

CROMWELL. His visits were... expensive.

CHARLES. But the hunting was good.

A pause.

CROMWELL. Your Majesty, only a few weeks ago the Army Council sent a messenger to you at Windsor.

CHARLES. Did it?

CROMWELL. You refused to see him.

CHARLES. I have no memory of that.

CROMWELL. You were repeatedly told he was waiting to see you.

CHARLES *shrugs. Another pause.*

Hunting is a great pleasure.

CHARLES. It is.

CROMWELL. Out on a chase, in woods, across streams. There's a kind of peace in it.

CHARLES. With companions you can trust. And speak to freely in the open air, away from walls and corridors.

CROMWELL. Yes. And God's bounty in nature all around.

CHARLES. The dream of a long, long chase.

CROMWELL. Suddenly you are in a forest clearing. And a stag is standing there, looking at you. And all is still. (*A pause.*) Your Majesty, if you had listened to my messenger at Windsor, we would not be buffeted about in these wrathful days.

CHARLES. 'These wrathful days.' You mean my illegal trial?

CROMWELL. The message was a proposal for a settlement between you and Parliament. Even in this dark hour.

CHARLES (*scoffs*). 'Settlement'? You think things can 'settle'?

CROMWELL. We were offering you your life!

CHARLES. Oh! Is my life in your gift?

CROMWELL. It would seem so. I wish it were not.

CHARLES. So do I. We are not just two men in the firelight, Master Cromwell. Not at all.

CROMWELL (*still for a moment*). Will you hear the conditions we offered, even now?

CHARLES. Somewhat late, is it not? Haven't I heard carpenters hammering, building some style of platform in the street?

CROMWELL. A few words from you, Sire, and the scaffold is firewood.

CHARLES. On your command?

CROMWELL. Yes.

CHARLES. Such power. Is it sweet?

A pause.

CROMWELL. Hear the conditions.

CHARLES. Excellent then, let us have conditions.

CROMWELL. First, that you cease to approach foreign powers to make war upon the country. In particular that you withdraw your appeal to Lord Ormonde and his Irish Royalists to invade.

CHARLES. Did I appeal to the Irish?

CROMWELL *takes out the intercepted letter to Lord Ormonde. He shows it to* CHARLES.

CROMWELL. You wrote this letter to Lord Ormonde.

CHARLES. I did not.

CROMWELL. You signed it.

CHARLES. Then I did. Or did not.

CROMWELL. There is your signature.

CHARLES (*not looking*). Well well.

CROMWELL. Come come, Your Majesty. This is a conversation that neither of us will ever acknowledge. Let us be frank.

A pause.

CHARLES. What else is in this 'settlement'?

CROMWELL. Land belonging to all the bishops will pass to the state.

CHARLES. Ha! To the rich grandees of the Army Council.

CROMWELL. No, to the people.

CHARLES. You be frank, sir.

A pause.

CROMWELL. Lastly, we propose that Your Majesty abandon your negative voice.

CHARLES. Ah. The heart of it. My 'negative voice'. You mean my right to veto any bill from Parliament. Without that, what am I?

CROMWELL. You would be the figurehead of the nation.

CHARLES. You mean stuck out on the front of the ship of state, like a painted thing. While you are the captain.

CROMWELL. The officers will captain the ship.

CHARLES. What? Elected by a crew of murderous sailors?

Anger is welling within CROMWELL.

CROMWELL. There will be a constitution. Of which you will be the guardian.

CHARLES. 'A constitutional monarch', what newfangled thing is that? The oil.

CROMWELL. Your Majesty?

CHARLES. The oil. At my coronation, I was anointed with holy oil.

CROMWELL. Ah.

CHARLES. Master Cromwell, they say you are a religious man.

CROMWELL (*scoffs*). Any man who says 'I am religious', is almost certainly not.

CHARLES. But you have been called 'godly'. Despite your… (*A wave of his hand.*) So understand, I was given a great burden. The oil made me King by the power of Almighty God.

CROMWELL. The oil's just a symbol.

CHARLES. No. It is the truth.

CROMWELL. The symbol of power.

CHARLES. No. It is the power. It is on me. Not all the water in the sea can wash it away.

CROMWELL. You see yourself as… a divine being?

CHARLES. I have a burden, sir.

CROMWELL. You believe God gave you power over all the rest of us because of a dribble of sticky stuff on your head?

CHARLES. Sir, were we to be civil tonight?

CROMWELL. Civil be damned, this is magic stuff, superstition! When will we be done with it? And stand with all our faculties in the clear light of day before God, all equal, all awake, all free?

CHARLES (*scoffs*). None of us is 'free'. We are chained to this fallen Earth in the places the Almighty gave us.

CROMWELL. You cannot believe that.

CHARLES. All I know is, when I was anointed, power over this land passed to me. Under me, the liberty of all my subjects is protected. Because they are, through me, under God. Through the crown. And the head that wears it.

CROMWELL. Dear God, man, do you think I want to execute the Lord's anointed?

A silence.

CHARLES. Your creatures wish it.

CROMWELL. I do not.

CHARLES. You acknowledge I was anointed?

CROMWELL. 'The Lord gave and he hath taken away.'

CHARLES. 'Naked came I out of my mother's womb and naked shall I return thither.'

CROMWELL. Book of Job.

CHARLES. Book of Job.

A pause.

CROMWELL. Sir, a head and a crown can fall into the dust.

CHARLES. And when king's head and king's crown are gone, what will be in their place? You?

CROMWELL. The people's Parliament.

CHARLES. Which you purged only fifty days ago. Because it voted to save me.

CROMWELL. We are all on a dark path.

CHARLES. Not I. I am in the light of Heaven, I am God's anointed and all is clear to me.

CROMWELL. Clear? Since you raised your banner against Parliament at Nottingham, what, seven long years ago, do you have any sense of what you have done to the Kingdom you claim is under you? The deaths, the mutilated bodies, the poverty?

CHARLES. Pish. Let them see how they fare under King Oliver.

CROMWELL *stands abruptly.*

CROMWELL. What happens is God's will. That is the evidence of His providence. Our victories against your armies showed the world the will of God.

CHARLES. Or the works of the Devil.

End of Scene Eight.

Scene Nine

The Court reassembles, CROMWELL *and* CHARLES *staying onstage to go to their places.*

CROMWELL *and* IRETON *are again sitting together downstage.*

COOKE. May it please Your Lordship, my Lord President. At the first session of the Court I read a charge against the prisoner containing the highest treason that ever was wrought upon England. That as King, he was guilty of a wicked design to introduce a tyrannical government, with himself at the head, in defiance of Parliament and its authority. The House of Commons, the supreme authority and jurisdiction of the Kingdom, here declares that the charge is true, as clear as crystal and as the sun that shines at noon.

CROMWELL. Now, even now, yield. Yield, man of blood…

IRETON. There is no more to be done.

CROMWELL. I believe even now the hand of God's mercy reaches out to touch his heart. He has only to feel it.

IRETON. His head is off, Oliver.

BRADSHAW (*to* CHARLES). Sir, now give a positive answer to the charge. If you do not, we will consider you guilty and proceed to judgement.

A long silence.

CHARLES. For me to acknowledge a court I have never heard of before…

Uproar.

CROMWELL (*to* IRETON). Off it is!

CHARLES. There is no law that says you can make your king a prisoner!

BRADSHAW. Sir, you must know the pleasure of the Court…

CHARLES. By your favour, sir…

BRADSHAW. No, sir, by your favour. You have written your meaning in bloody characters throughout the whole Kingdom. Clerk, enter a plea of guilty.

CHARLES. As Sovereign, I demand to speak to both Houses of Parliament. The King has the right to appear in Parliament.

BRADSHAW. You are only trying to delay.

CROMWELL. What is this?

IRETON. He does have that right.

CROMWELL. Tear out my eyes, grind my bones to dust, oh Lord! But make the man yield.

BRADSHAW (*to* CHARLES). Sir, if you speak to the Lords and Commons, there would only be delay of justice here. The Court is bound therefore not to grant your request.

A low murmur. CHARLES *does not react.*

The commissioners will now consider the sentence.

CHARLES. Shall I withdraw?

BRADSHAW. Sir, you will know the pleasure of the Court quickly. All they who find the prisoner guilty say 'aye'.

A silence.

CROMWELL (*low*). The cruel necessity. (*Aloud.*) Aye.

And 'ayes' come, at first ragged, then more together.

BRADSHAW. And who among you says 'nay'?

A silence.

CHARLES. Let me speak.

BRADSHAW. Sir, you are now to hear the sentence…

CHARLES. Sir, a word to you…

BRADSHAW. You denied we were a court. So it is not proper that you speak to us any more.

CHARLES. Well!

BRADSHAW. The sentence the law gives to a traitor, tyrant, a murderer and a public enemy to the country, that sentence you are now to hear read to you. Mr Solicitor General.

COOK hesitates for a moment, then he collects himself.

COOKE. For all the treasons and the crimes this Court adjudges, Charles Stuart shall be put to death, by severing his head from his body.

All the members of the Court stand. A hubbub of voices as the order of the Court breaks down. CHARLES *and* BRADSHAW *shout above it.*

CHARLES. Will you hear me a word, sir?

BRADSHAW. Sir, you are not to be heard after the sentence.

CHARLES. No, sir?

BRADSHAW. No, sir, by your favour. Guard, withdraw your prisoner.

CHARLES. Sir, hold your sentence!

The two TROOPERS *crowd* CHARLES. *The noise gets greater.*

BRADSHAW. All manner of persons…

CHARLES. I am not suffered to speak!

BRADSHAW. All manner of persons…

CHARLES. You will all be hanged, you will be torn to pieces! Your Parliament will never be sovereign!

BRADSHAW.…manner of persons that have anything else to do are to depart from this place.

End of Scene Nine.

Scene Ten

The scene of the trial, now empty but for CROMWELL,
IRETON, HARRISON, LENTHALL, BRADSHAW *and*
COOKE.

*The warrant for the King's execution is on the table. There is a
quill and an inkwell.*

BRADSHAW. Gentlemen. The warrant for the execution of His
    Majesty.

*He puts the document on the table beside the mace and the
sword. They stare at it.*

A pause.

IRETON. Are we the only ones here to sign? The law needs
    twenty.

CROMWELL. We will have more than that. All the
    Commissioners will sign.

HARRISON. I will call them in.

CROMWELL. No, we will sign first.

He takes the quill.

Come, my fellow regicides. Let us do this.

He signs his name. He hands it to HARRISON, *who signs.
He hands it back to* CROMWELL, *who hands it to*
LENTHALL.

CROMWELL *begins to giggle.* LENTHALL *signs and
hands the quill back to* CROMWELL. *He flicks the ink from
the quill at* IRETON. *They laugh.* IRETON *signs. He flicks
ink back at* CROMWELL. *They are laughing. He hands the
quill to* BRADSHAW *who signs and flicks ink at all of them.*
HARRISON *grabs the quill and flicks ink at* BRADSHAW.

*They are now corpsed by the occasion and their laughter is
out of control.*

COOKE *stands apart, stony-faced.*

(*Trying to stop laughing*.) Master Solicitor General, won't you sign?

COOKE. I am Prosecutor, I cannot sign. But I am content that I will be damned with you.

CROMWELL. Yes indeed, John Cooke.

CROMWELL *goes to him and they shake hands. He turns back. He and the others have not quite shaken off their laughter.*

Call the commissioners.

HARRISON. Gentlemen!

The stage fills with many COMMISSIONERS. [*Note. The warrant was signed by fifty-nine.*]

One of them – DANIEL AXTELL – steps forward. He shakes CROMWELL'*s hand.*

AXTELL. I thank God Almighty for this privilege today.

CROMWELL. Indeed.

AXTELL. Bless you in England's name.

He raises CROMWELL'*s hand and kisses it.* CROMWELL *pulls his hand away.*

CROMWELL. No! No, sir!

A silence, all still.

Then the COMMISSIONERS *turn, to become the crowd watching the final scene.*

Scene Eleven

The scaffold and the block high at the back. The
EXECUTIONER, *masked, with the axe. A* PRIEST.
TROOPERS.

HARRISON, IRETON, CROMWELL *come forward. They are
not watching the execution.*

Enter CHARLES, HAMMOND *with him.*

A gasp from the crowd, a swaying movement then they are still.

EXECUTIONER (*low*). I ask your forgiveness.

CHARLES. You do not have it, but in another world I will pray
for you.

He takes off his cloak and hands it to HAMMOND.

(*Low.*) Three shirts, Hammond, they must not see me shiver.

He kneels before the PRIEST *in prayer.*

HARRISON. The executioner told me he will not cry 'Behold
the head of a traitor.' He is afraid his voice will be recognised.

IRETON. No matter.

CROMWELL. What is his name?

HARRISON. Richard Brandon.

CROMWELL. He is with the Saints.

Enter FAIRFAX.

FAIRFAX. Gentlemen, may I join you?

CROMWELL. Of course, Thomas.

IRETON *takes out a timepiece and looks at it.*

IRETON. Now.

The four men kneel.

CHARLES. Is my hair to rights?

EXECUTIONER. It is, Your Majesty.

CHARLES. The block is too low.

EXECUTIONER. Bring the other block.

> *One* TROOPER *takes the block away, another* TROOPER *brings the new block.*

> CHARLES *looks down at the second block then looks up.*

CHARLES. A subject and a sovereign are clear different things. I tell you I am the martyr of the people.

> *He kneels and puts his head on the block.*

CROMWELL. Lord God of Hosts, be with England.

> *The* EXECUTIONER *raises the axe.*

> *End of Play.*